66 BOOKS BIG AND SMALL

84 INFORMATION BOOKS

102 KALEIDOSCOPE OF BOOKS

122 REPRODUCIBLE MATERIAL

Introduction

Writing and Making Books

Written by Moira Andrew

Published by Scholastic Ltd,
Villiers House,
Clarendon Avenue,
Leamington Spa,
Warwickshire CV32 5PR

© 1995 Scholastic Ltd
Text © 1995 Moira Andrew
234567890   6789012345

Author Moira Andrew
Editor Catherine Bywater
Designer Clare Brewer
Illustrations by Debbie Clark
Cover design by Lynda Murray
Cover photograph by Martyn Chillmaid
Designed using Aldus Pagemaker
Printed in Great Britain by Clays Ltd,
St Ives plc
British Library Cataloguing-in-Publication Data
A catalogue record for this book is available
from the British Library.

ISBN 0-590-53350-9

Contents

Think of a book as a precious object, complete in itself, portable, often beautiful and rich with colour. Think of a book as a companion in times of stress, filled with information, excitement, humour, emotion. Think of a book as a very personal link between writer and reader.

The home-made book, therefore, is one of the most personal documents we can possess, and for primary school children there are few activities which give the same sense of satisfaction as handling and reading a book which they have written and created themselves. It is a world away from the chore of the daily 'newsbook' or a writing task set in an exercise book. In a very direct way, the home-made book is a personal statement and turns child writers into authors.

Children involved in making and writing their own books practise their growing literary skills in a very practical and interesting way, mixing artwork with craft, creative writing with calligraphy. The result is a rewarding and enriching educational experience.

When the home-made book is finished it instantly becomes 'a precious object', not only to the child author, but to parents, friends and teachers. Like any published book, it can be read, admired or put away until later. It instantly acquires the magic of literature – that a reader can be informed or entertained even when the author is elsewhere. It is a permanent record of thoughts and ideas.

Because books can be about any subject in the world, teaching literary skills through the medium of making and writing books gives it value right across the curriculum. Children can be encouraged to make books concerned with maths or science; they can write books from an historical perspective or as if through an artist's eyes. They can make story books, books of poems, joke books; anything is grist to the young writer's mill – and every experience helps him/her towards becoming

fully literate.

In infant classrooms, book-making gives children a reason for writing and encourages independence. From their earliest days at school, children can be introduced to writing, often beginning with a single word on a page in a 'book' made from a folded A4 sheet. If the book is entitled *Clothes*, each page will have one word and a picture, for example 'jumper', 'trousers', 'shoes' – all the content being selected by the children. In addition to learning the mechanics of writing, these youngsters are also learning to read.

Such simple book-making provides a fresh start every time the child is presented with a new writing task. It offers everyone the chance to work on a clean new book, rather than a tired, dog-eared exercise book.

By the time children reach junior level, book-making encourages creativity and links artwork to writing in a very fundamental way. It helps to make the task of drafting and editing relevant and much more directly interesting, especially when the home-made book is an integral part of the exercise and they are keen to see it 'published'.

When book-making is used as an ongoing

method of teaching and learning and not simply a one-off activity, it allows the young authors to try out a variety of writing styles 'for real'. They can work on story, poetry, information, 'how-to' books and diaries with the knowledge that, when finished, their work will be permanent, not simply shut away in the pages of yet another exercise book.

This approach, when used consistently, gives children a sense of purpose and helps them to understand the concept of audience. It provides opportunities for them to use and develop the skills of design and technology in a very practical way and allows them to work on different scales, from mini-books to large anthologies and floor books.

Book-making encourages both individual and co-operative work. Often the children will want to write their own individual books, perhaps on a common theme, while at other times they might work together as a group to produce a magazine or newspaper. In the latter case, they must learn to share tasks and delegate responsibility, perhaps with one child taking on the role of editor.

Children must have an interest in all kinds of books before they are ready to make the most of their own book-making experiences. Therefore, it is important to make the entire topic of books familiar to them. Invite authors and illustrators into school so that children, having met the professionals, can become comfortable with the notion of themselves as authors and artists.

Finally, book-making is a complete educational experience for children; one which encourages them to think ahead, beyond the immediate writing task to the concept of a finished well-crafted article. When they are able to share with others a book of their own making – one which they have conceived and constructed, written and illustrated – it is a rare achievement, and surely the ultimate in communication.

From idea to printed page

Taking an idea through from the imagination to words on paper and eventually into book form is an exciting and exacting task. It requires from children the ability to combine words and pictures with the craft of book-making.

As in other areas of the curriculum, successful book-making and writing should be tackled in stages so that the end results match the children's developing capabilities. It can be a long-term activity, requiring the teacher's help and encouragement at every level, or one which can be completed quickly and easily. Either way, when a child's book is successful, children and teachers alike enjoy a tremendous feeling of achievement!

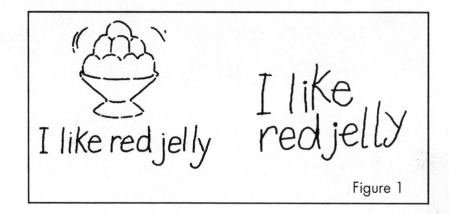

I like red jelly   I like red jelly

Figure 1

Getting started

With reception-class children it is important to emphasise constantly the links between reading and writing. Encourage the children to take pride in their work and try to make sure that they share the finished books with their parents.

Help beginners to have the confidence to make marks on paper. This leads gradually into meaning-making and eventually into 'real' writing. Let the children copy into their books from the chalkboard or from individual cards, always using whole words or phrases, so that their writing makes sense.

From the children's dictation write out labels for their pictures, gradually extending this into phrases and sentences so that it becomes a 'story'. The children should overwrite or copy directly into their books. (See Figure 1.)

At the next stage, the children can move on to using word books, a word bank or project posters, where words appropriate to their story topic are printed out. (See Figure 2 overleaf.)

As children move on to independent writing and book-making, they should be encouraged to use key-phonic. This means that they tune in to the first sound (or letter) of a

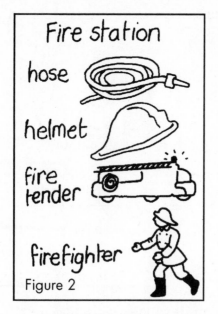

Figure 2

Figure 3

Moving on

At the next stage of book-writing, introduce drafting and storyboarding so that the children can begin to develop strategies for story-writing. Because many children find the task of drafting and rewriting a bit of a chore, encourage them to draft stories in note form.

One way is to give each child a sheet of A5 paper which should be folded in half to give a four-sided leaflet. This format is too small to take a full story, but large enough for a set of story notes. (See Figure 4.) On the first page the children should make notes about their characters and on

Figure 4

word. If they can work out the first sound for themselves they do not have to rely on your help every time. (The term 'key phonic' should be familiar to most teachers and is used throughout this book.)

Another method of encouraging independent writing is the use of the 'magic line'. If a child is stuck for a word, she should simply write the key letter and add a line. This allows the child's thoughts to flow and gives them more flexibility in their writing. Later, write in the whole word above the line and get the child to copy it. (See Figure 3.)

When helping children to make up poems and stories, it is important that they are encouraged to explore language. Don't let them settle for the first word that comes to mind. For example, if they are trying to describe the movement of a balloon, the first word they suggest will probably be *floating*. Get them to search for other words *(flying, drifting, blowing, hovering)* so that they begin to build a thesaurus in their heads. This skill can best be described as 'word-trading'. (See Shape books, page 30.)

Billy and James in the wood.

George the ghost. Billy and James run away.

Billy falls. He is crying.

The ghost says "Don't worry"

He takes the boys home.

"Good-bye George"

Figure 5

the next, the place in which the story is set. They should use the third page to rough out what happens and the last to suggest how the story will end. A draft of this kind gives the children a concrete outline to work to and confidence to see the task through, without having to write out the story twice over.

Story-boarding is another technique which helps children to work out where their story is going. They should rough out each scene in sequence, perhaps drawing pin figures and writing just a phrase or a snatch of dialogue under each picture. (See Figure 5.)

A more sophisticated method of working through a story is to set up an editorial conference. This means that a group of three or four children listen to one of their number reading his story aloud, and are encouraged to make helpful comments or ask questions about the way the story is going.

Word-processing

Most children enjoy the professional look that the use of a word-processor gives to their work, although undoubtedly it takes away the personal quality that is such a delightful characteristic of children's hand-written books.

In an ideal world, every child would have the opportunity to use the word-processor when he wished to do so. However, access to the word-processor is necessarily limited, so perhaps such a resource is best kept for those who find neat handwriting difficult and whose work never looks tidy. Children with learning difficulties also find use of a word-processor enables them to work at the same level as the others. They can dictate their ideas to a classroom helper and have the pleasure of seeing their stories printed out.

9

Audience

Child writers, at all stages, should be encouraged to think in terms of their intended audience. For example, books for younger children should use appropriate language, with repetitive phrases and clear illustrations. Brochures should contain accurate information and have the right amount of text on each page.

Encourage children to think about the needs of their audience, not only in terms of appropriate content, but in the style of their book.

The practicalities of book-making

Book-making and writing go hand in hand and, as the children's skills in writing progress, so they will want to use more sophisticated methods of making books. If the children begin working from the simple-fold and achieve success, then they will soon move on through zigzags and flap books to more complicated techniques.

To begin with, you might wish to prepare books ready for the children's use and have them all working to the same format.

Demonstrate different styles of book-making and as the children become more confident, suggest that they fold and cut the books themselves. Once they have practised the basic techniques, encourage the children to experiment.

As their skills develop, the children will want to choose and make books on their own, so designate a book-making table and lay out a range of materials so that they are easily accessible.

Materials

As well as a variety of paper (duplicating, cartridge, sugar paper and so on) and card in different colours and thicknesses, the children should have easy access to well-sharpened pencils, coloured pencils, felt-tipped pens and pens.

Make scissors (pointed, and for younger children safety scissors with rounded ends), paste and glue available, making sure the children know the 'house rules' about using scissors and that they know where to return them when they are finished.

If you wish the older children to use a craft knife, make sure that they know how to use it safely. Always ensure that they cut upon a self-sealing board.

The children will also need staples, plus ordinary and long-arm staplers. Make needles, cotton, coloured string, treasury tags, a hole punch and hole reinforcements available.

For special-occasion books, add to your range of materials shadowed paper, rainbow paper, day-glo paper and paper with fancy borders. Suggest that from time to time the children experiment with something quite different, for example using brown paper, greaseproof paper, wrapping paper or wallpaper.

Children will also enjoy making their own paper. Not only will they then have the satisfaction of writing and making books, but of making the paper as well! To make paper, tear up several sheets of newspaper into fairly small pieces and leave aside ready for use. Next, sprinkle about two handfuls of washing powder into a bucket of warm water and mix it well. Add handfuls of the torn paper to the mixture in the bucket and leave it for two hours until it is soft. Pour out any extra water and squeeze the mixture into a pulp. Beat the mixture with an egg whisk until it is really mushy, then transfer the pulp into a washing-up bowl and

stir it until it looks smooth. Sieve and drain the pulp, then tip a layer of pulp on to blotting paper or paper towels. Mould it roughly into shape with the flat of your hand, then put another sheet of blotting paper over the pulp and use a rolling-pin to squeeze out any excess water. Leave the pulp for several hours to start to dry out. At this point you can use an iron to give the finished paper a smooth appearance. Leave the paper to dry thoroughly. (This may take a day or two.) Peel off the blotting paper and trim the hand-made paper to the required shape. Hand-made paper will look quite grey and grainy. If you wish to colour it, add some powder paint to the mixture before beating it with the egg whisk.

Covers

There are as many different ways of making covers as there are styles of book. Sometimes the card or paper from which the book is made serves as a satisfactory cover.

To make a more substantial cover for a book designed to last, it is useful to teach the children how to tackle a simple turn-back card cover. For this you will need two pieces of card cut to the same size as the book pages, a sheet of cover paper 20mm bigger all round, some glue and a needle and thread. Figure 6 shows how the cover can be made and the pages bound in.

To decorate the cover, the children can experiment, using fabric and overlapping tissue paper. They can also draw or paint pictures, sticking them on to make a collage-style design. The children could also use magazine pictures or illustrations cut from seed packets, pasted down collage-style. These they can coat with a layer of thin varnish to give the covers a long-lasting découpage finish.

Another way of decorating book covers is to use marbled paper which can be made by mixing a litre of water with a little wallpaper paste in a paint tray, then when it sets, swirling oil paints over the surface. A sheet of paper can then be placed on the surface and quickly lifted off to give a marbled effect (Figure 7).

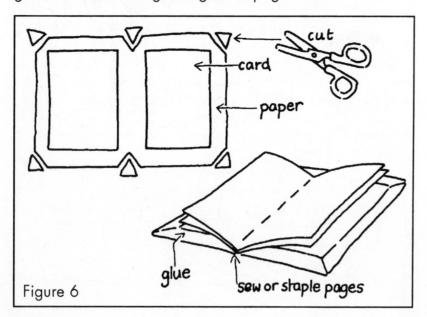

Figure 6

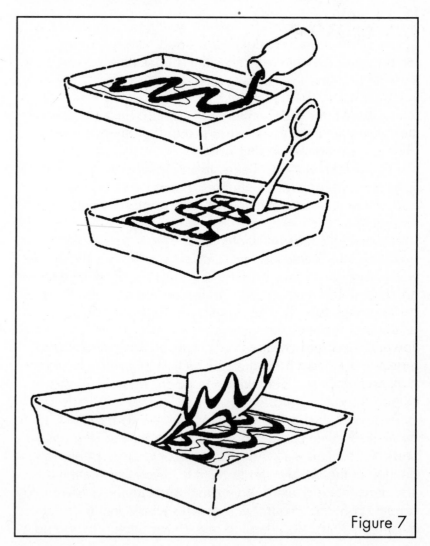

Figure 7

Book Week

When the children are confident about making and writing their own books, using the variety of writing styles and a range of book-making methods described, involve them in a major project for 'Book Week', one which will capitalise on their new-found skills of craftsmanship and inventiveness.

Take the children on an outside visit, for example to a forest trail, and afterwards discuss with them ways in which they might go about presenting the forest visit in book form. Encourage them to experiment and diversify, so that few of their books are alike.

Suggest that some children write and frame poems (see 'Under the sea', page 108), and some write adventure or mystery stories. Some can work together to produce a class book designed as a forest trail brochure with maps and background (see 'Going on school camp', page 92), what to look out for and so on. Suggest that they make books on flowers, trees and creatures of the woodland, mini-diaries, a growing zigzag and shape books. They could also make quiz books, pocket books, riddle books with flaps and comic strips, all on a common theme.

When the work is completed, make a display of the books and invite parents to the school to look, listen, read and admire. This encourages the children and would make a fitting contribution to Book Week, especially if the school invites a practising author along to enjoy the work on display and to congratulate the young writers and book-makers on their progress.

How to use this book

Having given some insights in this chapter into the different methods of teaching writing, the materials required and the practicalities of bookmaking, the following chapters provide a rich source of inspiration for making all types of book. Ranging from the very basic simple-fold, aimed largely at reception class children, through the fascination of shape books, zigzag books and books big and small, one arrives at the more advanced content to be found in the chapters entitled 'Information books' and 'A kaleidoscope of books'.

Writing and Making Books is intended as a pick-and-mix resource, rather than a resource to be read straight through. However, some infant teachers may wish to try out the idea of teaching reading and writing by means of book-making. The simple-fold, early zigzag and shape books suggested in this book will make it easier to follow a linked reading/writing curriculum through the infant years, stage by stage.

Other teachers may prefer to flick through the pages until they arrive at an idea that might be of value in their own classroom. There are sufficient ideas to occupy all stages of children, through from five- to eleven-year-olds.

There is no need to follow any of the suggestions slavishly. Each can be adapted to your individual circumstances, that is to your own pupils, year group and the resources available.

In the following chapters, several suggestions are followed through in detail and, in addition, most have extension ideas or another way to go about creating a similar book. Despite their common source, no two end results will look the same. Like the children they work with, primary teachers are immensely creative and inventive, capable of adapting and extending any of the ideas in this book.

Simple-folds

Simple-fold books provide an effective introduction to making books. They are easily put together, quickly finished and can be about things that interest even the youngest children. It is best to begin with one word per page folds, progressing to 'patterned writing' which may use a single repeated phrase, for example, 'I like' or 'I can'. However, both content and format can be adapted easily as children develop their reading, writing and book-making skills.

Of course, children's writing/reading abilities vary widely even within a single age group, but the standard simple-fold can accommodate a number of different levels of competence from naming words like 'sun', 'waves', 'jelly' through to quite complicated sentences such as, 'I like playing outside in the sun', 'I can splash in the waves at the seaside' or 'I think red jelly is the best'.

To introduce making a new book, take time to talk about the content with the children, beginning from the realistic basics of weather, pictures or objects which can be passed from hand to hand. Search for appropriate words with the children, questioning them, encouraging and explaining. The importance of this 'word-trading' cannot be over-emphasised as a way of helping to extend and enrich the children's vocabulary.

All the one-word or one-phrase folds suggested below require A4 duplicating paper, sugar paper or cartridge paper cut to A4 size. The better the materials the children use, the better the finished result will be, but duplicating paper is adequate for early book-making. Bought by the ream, it is reasonably priced and is available in a range of colours. In addition, the children will need ordinary and coloured pencils. Where additional materials are required, these are indicated under the heading 'What you need'.

The simple-fold is an easy book for children to make for themselves. As soon as they have become confident in the process, provide A4 paper, card, well-sharpened pencils, crayons etc. on the writing table and encourage the children to experiment in their own time. They should be allowed to write and draw, following the pattern you have established. They can write stories or rhymes or use the simple-fold book for non-fiction work. From their earliest days at school, the simple-fold can give young writers a feeling of almost instant success.

Look outside

Age range

Five to six.

What you need

Chalkboard, a set of weather symbols, weather chart.

What to do

A one-word simple-fold book about the weather provides an excellent starting point. It is something which every child can tackle at her own level.

With the children in a group around you, look out of the window and talk about today's weather, how it looks, how it feels. Talk about what children wear in different kinds of weather.

Talk about what children think is the best image to go with a particular type of weather, for example, they might think a picture of ducks or an umbrella is the best symbol for rain. Choose a symbol for today's weather and place it on the weather chart.

Figure 1

Introduce the four-page fold and show how it is made into a book (Figure 1). It may well be the children's very first self-made book, so make it a special occasion. Tell them that they are going to make their own book about the weather.

After discussion, write a single word about today's weather on the chalkboard, for example, 'sun', 'rain', 'cloud'. Tell the children what the word is and draw a simple picture to go with it.

Help the children to find the first page, keeping the fold to the left. Encourage them to copy the word and picture anywhere on that page. A few will say that they can't write, but praise and encouragement can work wonders!

Don't worry at this stage if the one word they write is a scatter of undifferentiated symbols across the page, perhaps accompanied by a scribbled picture. The important thing is they have attempted to link symbol to meaning. Take time with each child to read back what they have written, stressing the reading/writing association.

Complete the book over the next few days. The children will soon realise what to do and will carry home their first self-made book with considerable pride. If necessary, write any unclear word legibly beneath the children's attempts, so that parents are able to read the weather book with their child.

(It is useful to date the books. Keep one book for every month of the school year to help assess each child's writing progress.)

Follow-up

Ask children to bring in clothes suitable for cold, sunny and rainy days, then use them to make group or classroom displays with printed captions. Add books and pictures. Use these displays as a basis for simple-fold books on clothes for different types of weather. Again, keep to one word with one picture on each page.

Make more simple four-page fold books on other topics which are of interest to the youngest children – toys, food, pets, colours, fruit, flowers, birds and so on.

My family

Age range
Five to six.

What you need
Photographs of the family, magazine pictures, paste, scissors with rounded blades, ruler.

What to do
The family is perhaps the most popular topic among reception-class children and their teachers. Regardless of the make-up of individual families, all children are part of a tight-knit group and can relate to it. Talk with the children about who makes up the family (pet names, that Grandma is mum/dad's mum, that mum is both a mother and a daughter and so on).

Let each child choose a favourite photograph from home or select a magazine picture of an imaginary family. Ask them to tell the others in the group about the member of the family whose photograph they have chosen. Talk about the colour of their eyes, hair, about what they do, the name

Figure 1

they use for them, for example, Grandma can be 'Gran', 'Nan' or 'Granny'.

Make a four-page simple-fold for each child. Entitle it 'My family' and add the young author's name to the cover. Copy the title on the chalkboard and show the children that their books all have the same words on the cover. Look at their names and show that they use different symbols and are different in shape. Find children whose names all begin with the same letter. (It is important at this stage that children should begin to understand the difference between a letter, a word, a sound and so on.)

If possible, work with a classroom helper. Ask the children to think about one member of their family, getting the helper to write out the name with which the child is familiar on a scrap of card: 'Mummy', 'Mum', 'Grandad', 'Gramps' etc. Get each child to copy the name and draw a picture, perhaps using the photograph. Use a fresh page for each separate person in the family. As always, take time to read back what the children have written.

To make the simple-fold look like a photograph album, use a ruler to draw a frame round each portrait and let the children draw a pattern inside the frame.

Follow-up

Make a family picture gallery using the children's framed portraits, displayed under titles such as, 'Here are our mums', 'Here are our Grandmas' and so on.

Fix photographs (or photocopies of photographs) on the back of each portrait (using a temporary adhesive) and have a guessing game to see whether parents can identify themselves. They might get quite a surprise when they turn the portraits over to reveal the answer! Use a simple-fold book to make a family scrapbook with pictures cut from magazines. As before, let the children copy just one word to go with each picture.

Make a simple-fold book of the family of the Three Bears. (See Figure 1.)

My 'I like' book

Age range

Five to six.

What you need

Chalkboard or scraps of card, magazine pictures of food, food advertisements.

What to do

Discuss with the children what they like to eat. It is useful to have a number of magazine pictures or food advertisements to help with the discussion. (Greengrocers often are willing to give away posters advertising fruit.) Ask children why they like these favourite foods – colour, taste, smell. Who makes/grows/gives them these special things? Are there special occasions when we eat favourite foods – for example, parties, birthdays, Christmas, Diwali?

Prepare a simple fold for each child, using the front page as a cover. Print the title, *My 'I like' book*, and the child's name on the cover and ask the children to copy their own special food word, one to a page with an appropriate picture. Advertisements can be cut from magazines and pasted, scrapbook fashion, into the *I like* books.

Encourage the children to read and recognise the phrase 'I like'. Suggest they look for it in books on the library shelves.

Make more *I like* books about toys, flowers, fruit etc.

Follow-up

• Make jelly in the classroom with the children. Let the children write their own simple-fold recipe book entitled *I like jelly*. Each page should show one ingredient with words and a picture, for example, 'jelly cubes', 'hot water', 'leave to cool'. Try other simple recipes, for example, ice-lollies and uncooked sweets, and make simple-fold recipe books to go with them.

• Follow up with a book entitled *Things I don't like*, teaching recognition of the phrase 'I don't like'.

• Try making a *My 'I can' book*, for example, *I can run, I can skip, I can hop*. This is probably best done after a PE session in the hall or outside in the school grounds. Teach the phrase 'I can'.

• Make an *I'd like* book for Christmas, followed by an *I have* book in the New Year.

• Make a phrase poster to help common phrase recognition, for example, 'Once upon a time', 'One day', 'I have', 'I wish', 'Yesterday' and so on. Suggest to the children that they go on a 'phrase treasure hunt', matching the phrases they have learned with those in reading and library books. Children can work in pairs for this task, putting a phrase card in the books to mark the place. (See Figure 1.) Perhaps you might award a small prize for the best result, making sure that the winners are able to read back the phrases which they have found.

Figure 1

Open the door

Age range
Five to six.

Extension age range
Seven to eleven.

What you need
Fine card or cartridge paper, chalkboard or word cards, a key.

What to do
Show the children the key. Suggest that it might be a magic key and tell them a story about it – for example, it was found in the long grass, perhaps, on a sunny day. It opens a magic door which appears unexpectedly in the wall. Suggest in your story that this door exactly matches the height of each individual child – a magic door indeed! Discuss using the key to open the door in the wall.

Help the children to repeat the rhyme:
Open the door with the magic key.
Open the door and what do you see?

Teach recognition of the phrase, 'Open the door'. Suggest that animals are hiding behind the magic door. Ask the children to name some animals. If they come up with the fairly mundane creatures such as cats and dogs, suggest changes which could make them into magic creatures – not simply cats, but purple cats, striped dogs, silver cows and so on. Now look for a number to go with each idea – one

purple cat, two striped dogs, three silver cows and so on.

Write on the chalkboard: 'Open the door', then ask the children to copy the words on to the front cover of their simple-fold book. Add the picture of a door (it is not necessary to cut around the door as the front cover opens anyway). (See Figure 1.)

Ask the children to draw one purple cat (or whatever they have chosen) on the first inside page. On a card write out the text, 'one cat', for the children to copy. Those who are able to do so, might extend the text to 'one purple cat' and so on. Use one idea on each page, so that the book becomes a number book of magic creatures.

Figure 1

Follow-up
• Use the simple-fold door book to open on to a house, with one dad, one mum, three children.

• Make books incorporating gates, entitled *Come into the garden* or *Look over the wall*. Suggest making a simple-fold to go with each season, drawing a gate on the cover. For summer, try books entitled *Look at the flowers, Look at the butterflies, Look at the insects.* For winter, try *Look at the snow, Look at the bare trees, Look at the birds.* The children should use a new page for each new idea, with an appropriate picture and words as before.

• Make window fold books with a window drawn on the cover. Ask the children to suggest three things they can see by looking out of the window. Make a *Look outside and what can you see?* book, again using a page with words and a picture for each separate idea. Follow this with a simple *Look inside* fold.

- Make garage, shed or cupboard folds, again using the cover as an opening door. Ask the children to draw and label all the things inside.
- Ask the children to think of magic animals and mythical people. Make a list: dragons, ghosts, unicorns and so on. Encourage the children to elaborate upon the creatures, for example, 'green dragons roaring', 'purple ghosts flying', 'silver unicorns galloping', then make a book, taking a page for each idea, as before.

Extension
With children aged seven to eleven, suggest that they double the simple fold to make eight pages. Use staples to hold the book together. Make it into a 'disappearing door' book with each character going through an ever-smaller door on each page. Suggest that the children read *Alice in Wonderland*, then make their own version of the story.

Colour me

Age range
Five to six.

Extension age range
Seven to eleven.

What you need
A small collection of natural objects (each one a different single colour), a picture of a rainbow, a paintbox, chalkboard.

What to do
Bring in a collection of common natural objects, each one of a different single colour, for example, an orange, green leaves, a red tomato, pink strawberries, yellow primroses and so on. Talk about colours generally – the same colour, darker and lighter, different words for shades of green, red, yellow, etc. Talk about the colours the children are wearing, colours they can see from the window, colours in the paintbox, and colours in the picture of the rainbow.

Introduce the simple fold and ask the children to copy the words 'Colour me' from the chalkboard on to the title page. The children should draw an open paintbox beneath their writing. They should then draw a box shape on to each of the following three pages. Using a colour of their choice, they should fill in the first box. If they choose yellow, they should draw pictures of things that are yellow beside it – a chick, the sun, a buttercup and so on – so that they make up a 'yellow' page. Ask the children to talk about their drawings and get an adult to scribe the names of the various objects. Follow the same pattern for the other pages, using a different colour. Read the books with the children.

foil
raindrops

Extension

Older children can make colouring books for younger children using black outlines and a colour word on each page. When the pictures have been coloured, the juniors can scribe sentences for the infants and both can share in a paired-reading session.

The children will enjoy making a double-fold (eight-page) book called, for example *When Debbie painted a dragon*, using their own names. On page one they should write, for example, 'one green head' and draw an appropriate picture. On page two they should write 'two blue eyes' or 'four purple legs', illustrating each as they go. They should take a page at a time using a different colour for each part of the dragon's body until they reach the last page on which they might write something like 'and lots of bright red fire'!

Follow-up

The children can make a rainbow book using two simple folds stapled along the spine to give eight pages. Explain that they should draw a rainbow on the cover, then use each of the following seven pages to illustrate the colours of the rainbow in sequence. As in the *Colour me* book, the children should draw more objects which are always red, orange, yellow and so on. (Indigo and violet are more difficult, so here they might have to substitute coloured paint pots for some objects.)

To make an effective display of the finished rainbow books, paint and cut out a rainbow shape to pin across the corner of the classroom. Hang silver foil raindrops from it and display the books on coloured drapes (either on a table or pinned to a backcloth).

Who lives in the castle?

Age range
Five to six.

Extension age range
Seven to eleven.

What you need
Books and pictures or postcards of castles, chalkboard.

What to do
This simple-fold can form part of a topic on castles, or may be made after a visit to a castle. Show the children pictures of castles and point out special features, such as battlements, the moat, a drawbridge, arrow-slit windows and so on. Discuss people who might have lived within the castle walls, such as knights, ladies, jesters and servants.

Show the children that by turning the simple-fold so that it opens with the fold at the top, the cover can be made to look like a drawbridge. (See Figure 1.) Write the title *Who lives in the castle?* on the chalkboard and ask the children to copy it on to the cover of their book.

Work on a very simple text for each inside page, for instance 'a knight lives in the castle', 'a queen lives in the castle' and so on. Illustrate each sentence.

Follow-up
Use an adjective/noun/verb pattern to vary and extend the language used in the castle book. To do this, use the chalkboard to make a list of the children's ideas, working first on the nouns. Then extend the list left (for the adjective) and right (for the verb). It might look like this:

A royal king waving
A beautiful queen dancing

Figure 1

A funny jester laughing

Ask the children either to copy the ideas down or to make up their own, using the basic word pattern. Ask them to put one idea on each page of the simple-fold and illustrate it. As usual, encourage the children to read out their stories.

Extension
Let the children make humorous books about a haunted castle. Again, use the fold to give a drawbridge effect on the cover. The children can suggest a title, such as, *Enter the Castle – if you dare!* Discuss the sounds which ghosts/bats/skeletons might make. Again the children should give a page to each idea, for example 'The ghost goes WHOOOOOOOOOO!' 'The bats go SQUEEEEEAK!' They might bring themselves into the story at the end with, for example, 'But I go "BOOOOOOOOOO!" and chase them all away!'

All about me

Age range
Five to seven.

What you need
Photographs or self-portraits of each child as a baby and as they are now, paste, chalkboard.

What to do
This is another sure-fire topic for use with younger children, and one which fits in with work in science and religious education. Compare the photographs of individual children as babies and as they are now. Talk to them about how they have grown and changed. Talk about brothers and sisters.

Make a simple-fold for each child. Print 'All about me' on the chalkboard. Ask the children to draw a self-portrait and copy the title on to the cover. Suggest that the children complete the cover design by making a frame for their picture and filling it in with their own name, printed over and over again in different colours.

Help the children to paste in photographs or self-portraits on each page, preferably in chronological order. Use easy phrases, for example, 'Look at me', 'I am only six weeks old', 'Now I am two', 'Here I am the day I started school' and so on.

Follow-up
Bring in your own passport and discuss with the children how it is used. Show where your photograph is fixed and talk about the details inside. Look at where it has been stamped on entry to different countries. You might show the children where each country is on the globe.

Give the children simple-folds and suggest that they each make a passport for themselves. They should copy 'Passport to me' on to the cover, perhaps using a gold pen to make it

Footprints

David's bootees when he was one.

David's feet now he is five.

look impressive.

Inside they should include personal information, such as 'I have fair hair', 'my birthday is on 5th September'. On the last page they might include their likes and dislikes. Finally, they can paste in a recent photograph or add a self-portrait.

The children could also work together to make a large class book entitled *All about us* or *Look how we have grown!* Ask children to bring in some of their outgrown clothes and compare, for example, the size of baby bootees with the shoes they wear to school. Suggest that groups of children work together on this book, each contributing a garment and a line of text to accompany it. Ask a helper to staple the outgrown vest, socks or jumper on to the page. For example, the children can begin their book with baby bootees, perhaps writing beneath, 'Lucy's bootees when she was a baby'. On the next page there might be a pair of toddler's socks along with the text: 'David's socks when he was one', and so on. The children will get great pleasure from sitting on the floor 'reading' the finished book and it would add a tactile dimension to a topic on Growth.

I can dress myself

Age range
Five to six.

Extension age range
Seven to eleven.

What you need
A selection of children's clothes, a length of washing line or string, clothes pegs, scissors, foil, glue.

What to do
Hang a washing line at the children's level across the corner of the classroom. Ask a child to peg up clothes in the order in which he puts them on in the morning. Let one child from each group peg out clothes and discuss those which are easy or difficult to put on and why. Let some of the children demonstrate how they can do up buttons and zips. Put out a row of shoes and encourage the children to show how well they can tie laces and buckle shoes.

Give out simple-folds and suggest that the children make the cover into a wardrobe door, putting the title *I can dress myself* at the top. Ask an adult to help the children cut a doorflap and a hole in the door and back it with foil to make a 'mirror'. (See Figure 1 overleaf.)

On the inside pages the children can draw and write about the clothes they put on in order of dressing: 'my pants', 'my tee-shirt', 'my school skirt' and so on.

Follow-up
The children can make a going-to-bed simple-fold, beginning with 'I take my clothes off'. Then on the next page, 'I have my bath (or shower)'. Finally, 'I am in bed'. Turn the simple-fold so that the fold is at the top for this

Figure 1

idea, using the front and back covers as the bed. It should be neat and empty on the front cover; with a busy scene showing teddies and books and the child herself on the back. (See Figure 2.)

Extension

Suggest that the children make a simple- or double-fold diary of the day, showing different clothes worn for different activities, for example, shorts and tee-shirt for PE, trunks or swimming costume for swimming, play clothes for after school and so on.

The children can make a book showing the different kinds of clothes they wear at different times of the year. They can either draw them or cut out pictures from catalogues. Older children may like to write about the clothes they would like to have, rather than those they actually possess! Suggest a border design for each season's clothes; lots of suns and butterflies for the summer page, a border of falling leaves for autumn and so on.

Figure 2

People who help us

Age range
Five to seven.

Extension age range
Eight to eleven.

What you need
Chalkboard, clipboards and pencils.

What to do
This simple fold can go alongside RE work. Go round the school with a group of children. Encourage them to find out what jobs people do to keep the children safe, well-fed and warm. Find out something about the way the head teacher helps the children in school. Talk to the caretaker, crossing patrol person, cook, dinner lady, head teacher and anyone else who helps. The children should note down what they have learned, using either pictures or words.

Once back in the classroom, encourage discussion about what the children have found out. Write a list of names of people who work in school on the chalkboard, so that the children begin to recognise them.

On the cover of their simple-fold they should copy 'People who help us' and draw a picture of the school. On each of the following pages the children should choose which people they want to write about. The text can vary from the simple 'Mrs Green' with an accompanying picture of her to a more complex text, such as 'Mrs Green helps us. She makes our dinner'.

Follow-up
The 'people who help us' idea can be developed into a class book, each group taking different members of staff to

draw and write about. If the children have already made individual folds, they will be familiar with the names and will be able to 'read' the class book successfully unaided.

Encourage the children to extend their ideas concerning people who help them to those who work in the community. Firefighters, police officers, nurses, librarians and others can often be persuaded to talk to groups of children and to answer their questions. The children can make more simple fold books about these people who help them in day-to-day life.

Extension

Take children on a visit to the nearest shops and look at the goods displayed in the shop windows. Ask them to write or draw three things they could buy from each shop. They should also copy down the names of the shops.

Back in the classroom, the children can make either single-folds or a class book about the visit. They should put the title, *Down our street* or *We went to the shops* on the cover and, as usual, take a page to write and draw about a different shop. This will range from the name of a shop with a simple picture, for example, 'Post Office' or 'The Fruit Basket' to sentences like:
• We can buy newspapers, pens and books from Kiosks.
• We can buy stamps, cards and party poppers from the Post Office.
• We can buy apples, potatoes and flowers from the Fruit Basket.

The children can make an appropriate frame for each page showing flowers, vegetables and fruit for the fruit shop, pens, pencils and newspapers for Kiosks and so on.

The First Christmas

Age range
Five to six.

What you need
Illustrated books telling the story of the Nativity, stick-on stars, scraps of cloth, strong glue, card, scissors.

What to do
Tell the story of the Nativity. Discuss the various visitors who came to the stable. Look at the scraps of cloth and help the children to choose what they think might be appropriate for kings, angels and shepherds to wear.

Use fine card for this simple-fold as paper is unsuitable for collage-work of this kind. Suggest that the children turn the fold landscape-fashion to make a stable scene on the cover. They should write the title, *The First Christmas* and draw Mary, Joseph and the baby Jesus. Help the children to cut out scraps of cloth to make robes for Mary and Joseph.

The children should use the first inside page for a picture of the angels. They should cut out white lacy material to make the angel robes, then write simply, 'angels came' or use a more complicated structure, according to their ability. Let them stick lots of stars in the dark sky. On the next page ask them to write 'shepherds came', draw and make an appropriate collage, again with stars and finally, on the last page, write 'kings came'. They should use their brightest scraps of material for this collage.

This simple-fold makes a delightful gift at Christmas time.

Follow-up
Use the simple-fold for traditional stories which can be first told in class, then divided easily into three sections, for example, *Cinderella*, *The Three Billy Goats Gruff* and so on.

Shape books

Use a template and cut through several layers at once.

Figure 1

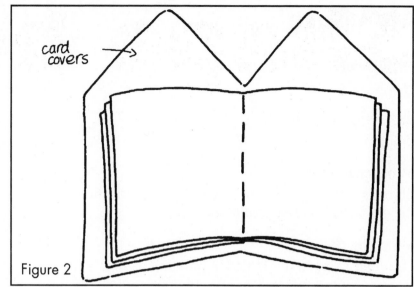

card covers

Figure 2

Children enjoy working on shape books. They find the idea exciting and, once they have become confident of their own skills, they vie with one another to invent new and different designs.

Shape books can be made on almost any subject area in the curriculum and it is a useful way to introduce topic work. Encourage the children to come up with their own suggestions once they have worked through some of the ideas suggested below.

For shape books based on the simple-fold, it is best to use cartridge paper as duplicating paper is not strong enough to hold a shaped outline. For books with several pages which are to be stapled or sewn along the spine, make the covers from fine card which is easy to cut, but fairly strong. The inside pages can be made from either cartridge or duplicating paper, cut to a rectangle, or shaped to match the cover.

The easiest way to mass-produce shape books for a group or class is to make a template cut from card. If you are making books with shaped inside pages, first fold both the card for the cover and enough paper to make the pages for one book. Use the template as an outline and cut through an entire book at one go. (See Figure 1.) For books with shaped covers only, trace round the template and cut several covers at once. Staple or sew each cover over the inside pages. (See Figure 2.) A golden rule for making successful books of this kind is to keep to simple shapes.

For the five- to seven-year-olds, it is perhaps best to cut out and staple the books ready for their use. When they are more confident of their book-making skills, the children will want to experiment with shape books for themselves.

To work on any of the books suggested below, the children will need pencils or pens for writing. They will also need wax crayons, coloured pencils or felt-tipped pens both for working on illustrations and for decorating the covers. Together with card and cartridge paper, these materials should be made freely available; they are not included under the 'What you need' headings.

My house

Age range
Five to seven.

Extension age range
Eight to eleven.

What you need
Scissors, staples or needle and cotton, a doll's house or picture of the interior of a house.

What to do
This idea helps to reinforce the beginnings of key phonic where children are learning to use 'key sounds', linking sound to the first letter of a word.

Use the doll's house or picture to introduce a discussion about different kinds of houses. Ask the children to think about what makes, for example, a bungalow different from a two-storey house or a farm house different from a trailer. You might introduce a bar chart showing how many children live in each type of house.

Discuss the different rooms in a house and the kinds of furniture we have in each. Introduce the words living room, kitchen, bedroom and bathroom, by writing them on the chalkboard and help the children to read and recognise them.

Make a house-shaped book with a card cover and four inside pages for each child. Suggest that the children draw a picture on the cover to make it look like their own house – get them to draw the correct number of windows, the door in the right place and give it their own house number and so on. They might also like to add a border of flowers. Tell them to leave a space to copy the words 'my house' or 'come into my house' from the chalkboard.

On each inside page of the book the children should write the name of one room at the top of the page, 'living room', 'my bedroom', 'kitchen' and so on. Ask the children to draw and name the pieces of furniture found in each

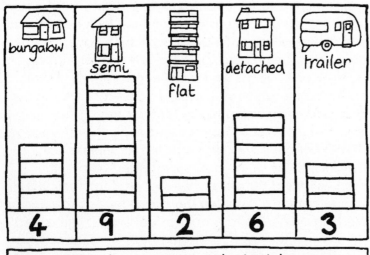

room of the house. Encourage them to use their emerging phonic skills for this task, either by simply using 'key sounds' to be completed by an adult scribe or by trying to sound out whole words.

Follow-up

• Make similar shape books entitled *Our school, The supermarket* or *The church,* encouraging the children to draw and name some of the things found in each building.
• Make a house-shaped book entitled *The house that Jack built* and ask the children to 'write' the story, using the 'draw and name' technique suggested above. They should take a fresh page as each new character is introduced.

Extension

Use a house-shaped book for a maths topic. To be really sophisticated, the children might work from actual plans, cutting the house outline to scale. They should work out the cost of buying carpets, wallpaper or paint and furniture for each room. They can paste in wallpaper samples and advertisements cut from catalogues to add to the overall effect.

The catalogues should give a rough guide of costs and the children can be 'given' a suggested sum of money from which to furnish their house. This will make them take decisions about how to keep within their cash limit.

The children could also make a class book, each group tackling a different room in the house. The idea also lends itself to making enlarged house-shaped displays cut to scale, each with its costs worked out and clearly displayed as part of the project.

Let the children write an adventure story about a haunted house. They should write the story on the left-hand page and provide an illustration on the right. Both the written work and the artwork should form part of the house-shaped design.

The surprise box

Age range
Six to seven.

Extension age range
Eight to eleven.

What you need
Two matching card circles, staples, a stapler, a small decorated box with a tiny model insect (spider, ladybird, bee) hidden inside.

What to do
Produce the little box with an air of mystery and show it to the children. In a dramatic tone of voice, suggest that a tiny magic creature lives inside. Encourage the children to think of the box as a home for a very little creature and talk first about what makes it different from the house they live in. They might think of such things as its shape, size, colour and pattern, that there are no doors and no windows etc.

Ask the children to suggest six creatures small enough to live inside the surprise box. Write a list of these creatures on the chalkboard, for example, ant, spider, beetle, worm, ladybird, butterfly.

Now ask for suggestions to describe the colour or pattern of each creature. Take time to explore suggestions with the children, looking for adjectives which suggest magic, i.e. not simply a 'black beetle', but a 'golden beetle', a 'shiny beetle', a 'tartan beetle', even a 'luminous beetle'. Write these words to the left of the list of creatures so that it reads 'a scarlet ant', 'a silver spider', 'a golden beetle' and so on.

Next, extend the list by writing to the right an appropriate movement verb, for example, 'a scarlet ant scurrying', 'a silver spider spinning', 'a golden beetle wandering' and so on. Encourage the children to search for unusual and different words, so that they begin to build a thesaurus inside their imaginations (this is described as 'word-trading' – see 'From idea to printed page' on page 6).

Give the children one card circle each. Ask them to write

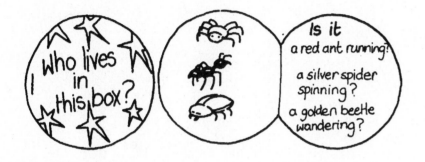

out their own list of four magic creatures, following the pattern on the chalkboard. Suggest that they borrow some ideas from the original list, but encourage the more confident writers to think of new ideas for themselves. The children can draw pictures of each creature they have written about.

Explain that the second circle will form the cover of the book – and the lid of the box! The children can use a question for the title, such as *Who lives in the surprise box?* or *Can you guess who lives here?* Ask them to decorate the cover with an overall pattern and finally staple the lid over the writing so that the reader has to 'open the box' to read the story. (See Figure 1.)

As an alternative, avoiding the use of staples, the book can be made from one sheet of card folded over, with a

Figure 1

circle outline drawn and cut almost to the edge so that it makes a hinge. Some children may be able to make this style of book for themselves.

Of course, you should open the box at the end of the lesson so that the children can find out what is hiding inside – although the children are unlikely to let you forget to do this!

Follow-up

• Make a book in the shape of a treasure chest with a lid. The children can write a story called *Pirate Treasure*. Suggest that pirates have found a battered chest and that they open it hoping to find treasure. Ask the children to guess what that treasure might be. Encourage them to tell the story, using the adjective/noun/verb word pattern shown above, for example, 'a golden coin shining', 'a precious jewel shimmering'. Tell the children to design the cover as a lid, so that the story is hidden until the 'lid' is opened.

• Make a holiday book shaped like an opening suitcase called *My summer holiday*. Provide four inside pages to tell the story; for example, the first page could read: 'I took pink-spotted pyjamas.' The children should write or copy the sentence and draw a picture to match. They should then take a new page for each new item taken until they come to the last page which might read, 'Guess what I forgot? I forgot my..............' (the children will supply the word).

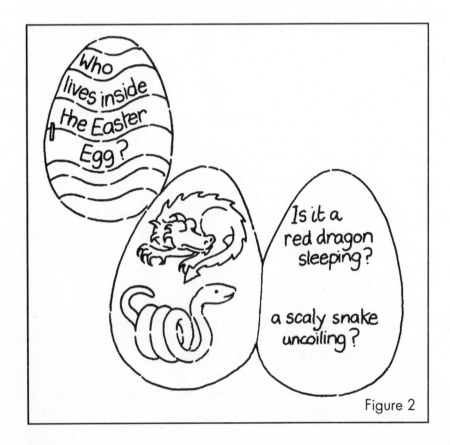

Figure 2

• Make an egg-shaped Easter book, again using the cover as a lid. The children can use the word-pattern as before. They might suggest 'a red dragon sleeping', 'a scaly snake uncoiling' and so on. Alternatively, the children could make the cover open along a cracked line in the centre of the egg-shape and staple it at each side. (See Figure 2.) (See also 'Who grows inside an egg?' on page 44.)

Extension

The surprise box idea can be extended for more experienced writers. Show the children the decorated box and suggest that it is a 'Box of colours', or a 'Box of wishes' or a 'Box of sounds'.

To work on the 'Box of colours' idea, ask the children to imagine opening the lid of the box and seeing all the colours of the world spill out. Encourage them to explore exciting ideas of what the colours might be and where they have come from – blue hauled from the depths of the ocean, purple snipped from a rainbow, black dug from holes in space etc.

Ask 'open' questions to help the children develop their ideas. What textures would the colours have? Would they be like paint? Like flowers? Like the silks saris are made from? What would mum say if the colours spilled all over the bedroom carpet? How would the caretaker react if the colours spread across the classroom floor?

List some of the children's ideas on the chalkboard and suggest that they borrow some, if necessary, to begin their poem or story. Ask them to work first on a rough draft and when it is ready for transcribing into 'best' work, write it into the pages of a book shaped like a round box, again making the front cover into a decorated 'lid' which has to be opened to reveal their writing.

A similar method can be used for stories or poems centring on the idea of a 'Box of wishes' or a 'Box of sounds'.

What can you do with a ball?

Age range
Five to seven.

Extension age range
Eight to eleven.

What you need
Card circles, (for the covers), matching paper circles (for the pages), staples, a stapler, a tennis ball.

What to do
Prepare round-shaped books with card covers and four paper pages. Staple them together at one side.

Ask the children to close their eyes and pass the tennis ball around. Then encourage them to look at the size and texture of the ball. Does it bounce? What is it made of? What games can they play with it?

Use the children's answers to make up a word pattern, for example, 'I can kick a ball', 'I can throw a ball', 'I can roll a ball', etc. Explain that they should write a sentence and draw a picture for each page.

More able children could be asked to extend the word pattern, for example 'I can kick a ball', 'I like to play football with my dad.' Again, they should take a new page for each new idea and draw an appropriate picture.

The children should print the title as a question, *What can you do with a ball?* They can decorate the remainder of the cover in thick wax crayons to make a bright beach-ball pattern.

Follow-up
The children could be asked to bring in a selection of balls to make a table display. They might grade them from the smallest (a marble) to the largest (a beach ball), and from the heaviest (a medicine ball) to the lightest (a table tennis ball). They should then make another round-shaped book about different kinds of balls: footballs, cricket balls, golf balls.

Extension

To introduce the idea of image, explore with the children as many other things as they can think of which are shaped like a ball, for example, the sun, the world, an orange. The children should write short stories or poems based on this idea.

They might write:
The world is like a coloured ball,
bouncing through space.
Throw it and it will roll
round and round, twisting
across the Milky Way.

Ask the children to make up several poems using this pattern. Write them in round-shaped books and display the books in linked circles as in Figure 1.

The children can also use round-shaped books in which to write a *Book of Inventions*, suggesting crazy ideas for using a ball, for example: designing a new planet, making a giant's eyeball, inventing an unmeltable snowball and so on. They should describe how their inventions can be made

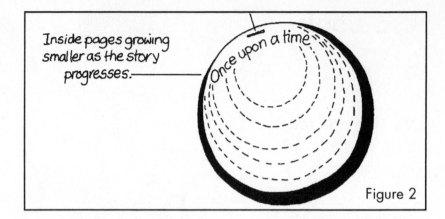

Inside pages growing smaller as the story progresses.

Once upon a time

Figure 2

and ten things they can do with them so that it becomes a ball-shaped joke book.

Older children could write an adventure story which takes place in a deep dark hole or inside a tunnel. The story should involve a search. They should use black card cut into circles for the covers, stapling round pages inside the book. These pages could become smaller and smaller as the story develops, so that the reader has the impression of falling into a hole as the book is read. (See Figure 2.)

What can you do with a ball?

Figure 1

ABC book

Age range
Five to seven.

Extension age range
Eight to eleven.

What you need
Scissors, a variety of alphabet books, an alphabet frieze, magazines, glue, scissors.

What to do
Look first at the alphabet frieze with the children. Talk about the names of letters and their sounds. Play an 'I spy' guessing game to help children become familiar with the concept of 'key' sounds (as in key phonic). Talk about children's names and group together those whose names begin with a particular letter or sound.

Look next at a range of ABC books with the children. Talk

about animals or toys which all begin with a particular letter of the alphabet. This activity helps to reinforce the notion of key phonic which is an important tool in independent writing.

Prepare a large class book, shaped around the linked letters ABC, as in Figure 1. The children should work in groups, each taking a different letter of the alphabet to illustrate, and writing captions for the pictures they have drawn. Children working on the 'A' page could choose animals (ants, adders, antelopes and so on), or they could choose to illustrate random words, all beginning with the letter A (apple, arrow and so on).

Alternatively the children could use pictures cut from magazines.

You may also wish to make and give out individual ABC-shaped books, so that each child can work on a book of his own.

This activity can be spread over a number of sessions until Z is reached.

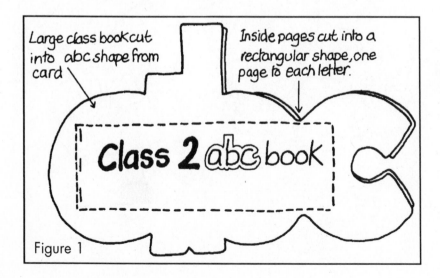

Large class book cut into abc shape from card

Inside pages cut into a rectangular shape, one page to each letter.

Class 2 abc book

Figure 1

Extension

Work with the children on alliterative phrases, one for each letter of the alphabet, to make up individual ABC books, for example: angry alligators abseiling, batty badgers bouncing, zany zebras zipping. This is an excellent exercise to help with dictionary work. (X will be difficult, so allow some cheating here! For example, exotic xenurus exercising.) If the children are fairly experienced in book-making, they could be encouraged to make their own ABC books, again shaped around three linked letters, perhaps XYZ for a change.

Write animal story ABCs using as many words beginning with one letter as the children can find. Let the children work in pairs or groups for this project, making up a sentence, writing it down and passing it on. For example, they may think of something like, 'Amy the ash-blonde armadillo had lived all her life in America. One day Arthur..............' The next group should continue the story, again using words beginning with A. Of course, if all the groups are working on the project at once, they may be writing an 'A' story, followed by a 'T' story and so on. This activity will give rise to much hilarity, and it will help to familiarise the children with the use of a dictionary.

Put each story into its own letter-shaped book, so that you end up with a book for each letter of the alphabet. The children should aim to make their stories as funny as they can, while still making some kind of sense. The authors can then read their stories to younger children.

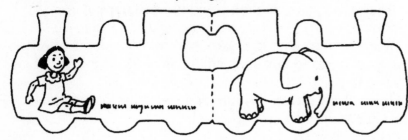

Our school trip

Age range

Five to eleven.

What you need

Scissors, paste, photographs or brochures of the place you are intending to visit, maps of the route.

What to do

This activity should be linked to an outside visit to a castle, farm, forest trail or such like. It is useful to set the scene for the children by sending off for pictorial or printed information beforehand. Some of this material can then be used as a basis for book-making.

Before the trip, talk with the children about where they are going, dates of the trip, what they need to bring with them, how they will be grouped, etc. Use this discussion as a briefing session and show the children the brochures and photographs of the destination. Look at a map with the

children and trace the route the coach will take. Help the children to make a route map for a wall display.

Help each child to make a book made from a bus/coach template with card covers and paper pages cut to fit the bus outline. Show them how to draw window outlines on the cover of their book, printing a suitable title underneath, for example, *Our school trip* or *Off to Alton Towers*. They can then draw, colour and cut out individual figures waving and glue these into the window spaces. (See Figure 1.)

Across the first two pages, give the children the opportunity to make a simple version of the route map, marking the main places of interest that they should look out for. If they know something about these places in advance it will provide something interesting for them to do on a long journey.

On the next page suggest that they make up a menu for their lunch boxes, drawing and naming healthy foods. On the following pages the children can write and draw 'What I most want to see' and 'Questions I want to ask'. This will help to set out an agenda for the visit.

The second part of the book can be completed after the trip as a record of the visit. Discuss aspects of the visit with the children, what they thought was the most interesting part, most exciting part, and so on. They should then take a separate page to draw and write about, for example, 'The funniest thing that happened', 'The most marvellous thing I saw' or 'What I'm sorry I missed'.

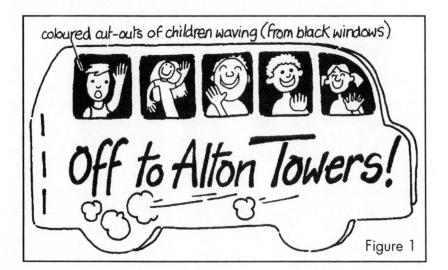

coloured cut-outs of children waving (from black windows)

Off to Alton Towers!

Figure 1

Welcome to our school

Age range
Five to eleven.

What you need
Your school brochure or information leaflet, a plan of the school if one is available, chalkboard, camera.

What to do
Make a simplified outline of the school building, tall and thin for a two-storey school, squat and wide if your school is a low modern style etc. Use the template to make individual books with card covers and paper pages cut to match. Children who are experienced in book-making should be encouraged to make the books for themselves.

Take the children outside and let them draw in details of doors and windows on the cover of their books. Remind them to leave a space in which to print the name of the school.

Once back in the classroom, ask the children what they think makes their school special. Their friends? The teachers and other people who work there? The uniform? Things that happen at different times of the year, for example, Harvest Thanksgiving, Christmas play?

List some of the children's ideas on the chalkboard and suggest what information the children might give on each page and how they should go about it. For the uniform page, they might draw and name items, showing the school tie, sweatshirt, PE kit etc. On another page they can draw portraits of their friends, with their names printed below, inside a patterned frame, and so on.

Look at the school plan with the children and help them to trace their way from the caretaker's room to the front door, from the kitchen to the head teacher's room etc. The children might draw a simplified version of the plan across a double-page spread in their books.

Again, using the plan, the children can find their way round the school, looking into rooms which they don't themselves use. Suggest that they look for something special in each room and later discuss with them some of the details they have noticed.

Once back in the classroom, younger children can take a page at a time to write about and draw each room they have visited. They can use patterned writing, labelling the pictures 'This is me in my classroom', 'This is Mrs Noble's classroom', 'This is Mrs Green's kitchen' and so on.

Older children can be asked to work in groups to find out three things about every class, for example the teacher's name, classroom number, age of the children. Now ask them to find out something special about each class. It might be along the lines of:

- Surinder's little sister is in Mrs Webb's class.
- I like the rainbow picture in Mrs Thompson's room.
- Mr Davies lets his children use felt-tips.

Of course, the children can expand on this information if they wish.

The children at the top end of the school could be asked to produce a brochure for parents of new children coming to the school for the first time. Discuss with them what kind of information the parents might need; for example, school times, cost of dinners, school uniform, school rules (and why the rules are important). Encourage them to add drawings and pen portraits of each teacher, a plan of the school, a personal piece about their own first day in school, the best-ever day in school, the funniest/saddest thing that has ever happened to them and so on. This information should be presented in a school-shaped book.

Let the oldest children make a school-shaped book suitable for the newcomers themselves. Discuss with them what they would have wanted to know when they first came to the school and how they can present the book for non-readers. This is a wonderful opportunity to write for a real-life audience. Let the children take photographs, so that the newcomers (their readers) can identify people and places around the school.

Who grows inside an egg?

Age range

Five to seven.

What you need

Books cut ready in an egg shape, pictures of chickens hatching, an egg.

What to do

Sit the children in a group and show them the egg. Let them pass it carefully from hand to hand. Talk about the chick that hatches from an egg and look at pictures of chicks. Discuss with the children other creatures that hatch from eggs – snakes, birds, crocodiles, turtles, perhaps dragons?

Ask the children to take on the curled-up shape of a creature inside an egg. (This is a good task for a PE/dance session.) Then ask them to uncurl, stretch, crack open their 'egg' and finally step or crawl out.

Give the children the egg-shaped books and explain that on the first right-hand page they should draw a chick curled up, on the next a crocodile, a snake and so on. Explain that

they should leave the left-hand page blank as this will be used for writing. The youngest children may simply name the creature, those who are more capable can write an appropriate sentence, for example, 'A snake grows inside an egg'. On the last page they can draw and write about a dragon, letting their imaginations run riot!

Decorate the cover with speckles (as for a bird's egg) and print the title *Who grows inside an egg?* across the middle. (See Figure 1.)

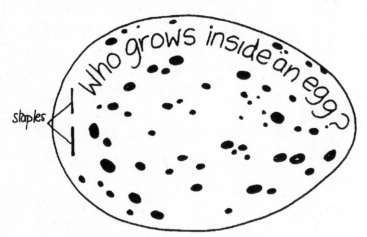

Figure 1

Around the year

Age range
Five to eleven.

What you need
Fine card, scissors, copies of photocopiable pages 123 to 126, chalkboard.

What to do
Take every opportunity to make shaped books for the annual festivals celebrated in school. On each occasion talk with the children and discuss what the festival means. Encourage them to think of words appropriate to the festival and write them on the chalkboard or, for the youngest children, make a wall poster of the words to which they can refer as they write. Help the children to draft ideas for suitable content and make shaped books. Use the template outlines on pages 123 to 126 for the youngest children. Older and more experienced book-makers might make their own books shaped appropriately to the festival, for example:
• Harvest Thanksgiving: books in the shape of an apple, basket, cabbage, loaf of bread;

• Hallowe'en (if it is celebrated): books in the shape of a turnip or a pumpkin;
• Diwali: books in the shape of a candle or lantern;
• Bonfire Night: books spiked at the top like bonfires, rocket-shaped books;
• Remembrance Day: books with red card covers and shaped like a poppy.
• Christmas: for the Nativity story make books in the shape of the stable or manger. Try also stocky, person-shaped books to tell the shepherd's story, the kings' story, the angel's story. For the secular side of Christmas, make books shaped like a chimney, a stocking, a brightly-decorated parcel, a Christmas tree, a Father Christmas figure;
• Chinese New Year: books shaped like fish kites;
• Pancake Day: books shaped like a frying pan or a lemon; inside write out a recipe for lemon pancakes;
• Valentine's Day: make a heart-shaped book of poems;
• Easter: books shaped like an Easter egg.

Genie in the bottle

Age range
Seven to eight.

Extension age range
Nine to eleven.

What you need
A selection of bottles of different size and shape (scent and bath products are the best), a silk scarf, an illustrated book telling the story of Ali Baba.

What to do
Introduce a touch of magic into the session by hiding one of the bottles behind a silk scarf and discussing the concept of magic with the children. Find out if the children know any traditional fairy stories. Look at the stories of Cinderella, Aladdin, Sleeping Beauty, Beauty and the Beast and Ali Baba. Talk about what a magician does – perhaps using television magic shows as a starting point. Talk about magicians in stories.

Reveal the bottle and tell the story of *Ali Baba*. Ask for suggestions as to how the children would call up a genie. What would he look like? What would they say to him? Ask the children to imagine what they would wish for, given the traditional three wishes. Try to steer them away from the visit to Disneyland syndrome and instead to think of magical ideas – to slide down a rainbow, meet King Neptune, ride on a magic carpet and so on.

In a bottle-shaped book with several inside pages, let the children write an adventure story in which they rub a bottle, a genie pops out and they are given three wishes. Encourage them to make it as exciting and other-worldly as they can.

Extension
Suggest the same idea, but in a different context. For example, in RE or environmental studies the children could discuss what would make the world a happier place. Discuss what we could do for people affected by famine or war. Suggest that they choose three wishes to bring peace and plenty to the world.

For those children interested in environmental issues, choose three wishes to save the whale, seals, rainforests etc. Look at materials produced by World Wildlife Fund, Oxfam etc. for source ideas. The children should write out their ideas in either class or individual bottle-shaped books.

Show a decorated top using a silver or gold pen.

The Three Wishes

Dark blue or green.

By Katie

Space adventure

Age range
Eight to eleven.

What you need
Books and photographs about space travel.

What to do
Discuss with the children the difference between our scientific knowledge of space travel and ideas in science fiction. Ask the children to choose which kind of writing they would like to tackle; a space adventure fantasy or factual information on space travel. Pair the children, as far as you can, so that a fiction writer works with one who is interested in producing an information book. Ask them to exchange ideas orally and to make some rough notes.

The children should plan and draft in the usual way, with each pair finally producing two rocket-shaped books, one pure information, the other telling a science fiction adventure.

Treasure islands

Age range
Eight to eleven.

What you need
Maps, books and brochures about faraway places.

What to do
For this book, children can design their own treasure island with caves, sea monsters, treasure chests, sunken ships and so on.

This writing task demands detailed planning and the children should be encouraged to draft their ideas in note-form before they settle down to working on the final story.

Ask the children to make the books with an island outline. Explain that they should map out all the special features on the cover, along with the title, *Treasure island adventure*, and the author's name. They should write an adventure story which provides clues for the reader to follow, each page bearing the next part of the story and yet another clue. The author should lead the reader along one path after another, finally arriving at a most unexpected conclusion.

Follow-up
Ask the children to design a holiday brochure to entice visitors to their own special island. Stress that they should make it a very exciting place with lots to do. They should provide pictures of the beaches, forest trails, visits to the caves and shipwrecks. Ask them to suggest ways of travelling to the island and give an idea of accommodation and how much the holiday will cost. (The children can look at holiday brochures to find out the special style of writing used.)

Zigzag books

Zigzags provide a style of book-making which lends itself to a continuous story or to a sequential piece of writing where children aim to describe such things as seasonal change or a growth pattern, for example, spawn to frog.

To make the simplest zigzag book, use a sheet of fine card or cartridge paper, approximately 600mm x 200mm. Holding the paper lengthways, fold it in the middle, then fold each side back on itself to make a concertina shape. (See Figure 1.)

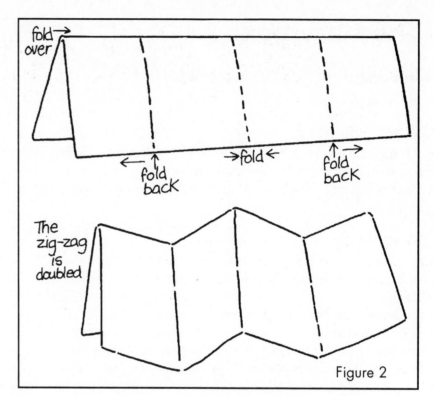

Figure 2

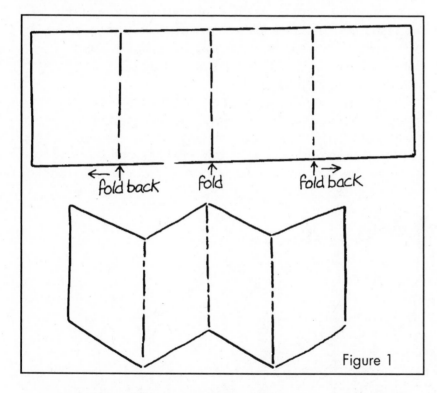

Figure 1

To make the zigzag more sophisticated, use the sheet doubled, keeping the fold at the top, then fold it in three places, as before. (See Figure 2.) This will allow you to cut flaps or holes where a picture or an unexpected turn in the story can be hidden. Young children enjoy raising the flaps to reveal secret pictures or messages, so it is an ideal way of presenting stories when older children are asked to write for beginning readers. (This format is referred to as a 'double zigzag' in the text.)

The zigzag is a very versatile format, easy to assemble and useful through all stages of the primary school. Two zigzags can be taped together at the back to make a longer thicker book, if necessary. As they are free-standing, zigzag books can be used to form part of a table display.

To make any of the books outlined in this section, the children will need card, cartridge or sugar paper for the book itself, pens or pencils for the text and felt-tipped pens or pencil crayons for the illustrations.

The story box

Age range

Six to eight.

What you need

An attractive box containing four interesting models (for example, a bee, a flower, a jewel, a castle), a four-page double zigzag, scissors, chalkboard or personal word book.

What to do

To help young children write a story with a number of characters in zigzag format, the 'story box' is a useful device.

Gather the children around you and suggest that a story is hidden inside the 'story box' and that there is no way of telling the story until the children themselves make it up. Produce the first character from the box, the bee, perhaps.

Encourage the children to look at the 'coat' the bee is wearing and talk about its colour and pattern. Ask them each to think of a name for the bee, for example Betty Bee, Buzzy Bee, Boris Bee. Start off a story for the children, for instance, 'One sunny morning Boris Bee woke up. He put on his stripy orange and black coat and buzzed off to look for adventure.' Ask the children to suggest where he went, how he moved, what he was looking for, and so forth.

Then take out the flower (discuss appropriate descriptions – red as 'blood', as 'fire', as 'a ruby'), and say that this is where the bee landed. Ask the children why. They may suggest it was because his wings were tired, because he lost his way, because he was looking for honey, and so on. Help the children to build up a story bit by bit, introducing next the jewel, then the castle.

Once they are happy with the way the story is going, suggest that the children write their own story on the four inside pages of the prepared zigzag, taking a page for each part of the adventure. In this way, the children will feel that they are in control of the story and that they can reach

a satisfactory conclusion. The ending is often difficult for inexperienced story-writers. By using the 'story box' device every child has some knowledge of what goes on each page and of where the story is leading. Although all the children begin from the same set of characters, every story will be different!

Help the children with each separate part of the story as necessary, perhaps by putting the words they need on the chalkboard or into their personal word books.

On the last page, the children may want to hide the ending behind a flap. If so, let them draw round a small box as a template. You may need to help the children cut open the flap, remembering, of course, to leave a 'hinge'.

Follow-up
Once the children are familiar with the story-box procedure, introduce them to a variety of different characters from which they can make up new adventure stories for themselves. Perhaps you could place four new characters on the writing/book-making table each week and encourage the children to use them as starting points for individual work.

All aboard!

Age range
Five to seven.

Extension age range
Eight to eleven.

What you need
Zigzag books – at least four pages in length, with the covers making six in all (see Figure 1), scissors, paste, books or pictures of trains.

What to do
This book might be made as part of a topic on transport. Discuss with the children different kinds of transport, and

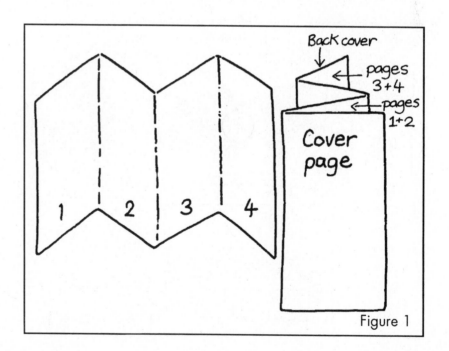

Figure 1

talk about how they travel when they go on holiday. Ask if anyone has ever travelled by train and talk about the sounds of trains, where the nearest railway station is, what special clothes train drivers and other personnel wear as part of their uniform, and so on.

It might be possible to take the children on a visit to the local station, on a short train journey or, even better, on one of the steam trains run for tourists and railway enthusiasts.

Give out the zigzag books and show how they divide into sections or pages. Talk with them about ideas for making it a storybook train, suggesting that they can decide for themselves where it should go and who will go with them. Ask the children to draw and cut out four nursery rhyme characters, a train driver and a guard. They should paste the cut-out nursery rhyme characters on each inside page with a line of writing, for example 'Little Miss Muffet is off to Blackpool'.

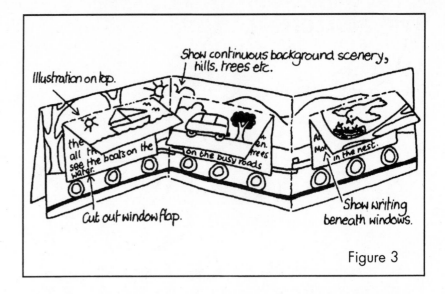

Figure 3

Figure 2

The children should make the first turned-back page into a cover, drawing the engine and pasting on the engine driver figure. Tell them to add the title, *All aboard!* The guard can be pasted on to the last turned-back page, making six pages in all. (See Figure 2.)

The youngest children can make the train zigzag into a simple counting book. They should draw, for example, one elephant on page one, two tigers on page two and so on. This will give a book which goes up to five, using the front cover for the title and the last page for five animals.

Extension

The children should draw windows and cut flaps in the four inside pages of a double zigzag to make 'windows'. Behind the flaps they should write about all the things they can see from the windows; on the flaps they should illustrate what they see. (See Figure 3.) This idea works really well if the class has been on a real train journey. Again, by drawing, they should make the front cover look like the engine of the train, the last like the guard's van.

The butterfly's story

Age range

Five to seven.

Extension age range

Eight to eleven.

What you need

Pictures and information books on the life cycle of the butterfly, simple zigzags.

What to do

Make zigzag books with the children, ensuring that there are four inside pages available.

Look at butterfly pictures, or even better, take the children outside to look at real butterflies and caterpillars in the school garden. Discuss with the children the stages of a butterfly's life cycle – from egg to caterpillar, from caterpillar to chrysalis, from chrysalis to butterfly.

In their zigzag book the children should draw and name each of the four stages of the butterfly's life. From pictures, they should choose a particular kind of butterfly, Tortoiseshell, Red Admiral, Painted Lady etc., and try to copy the pattern accurately on to the front cover of their books.

Extension

Older children should make an eight-page zigzag, making notes on each stage of a butterfly's life cycle on the left-hand page, illustrating the right, so that it becomes a nature notebook.

The older children can use the same format to work on the life-cycle of a frog, a toad, a dragonfly or a moth. Again, they should make notes and try to reproduce the information as accurately as possible, combining the skills of a scientist for the notes with those of an artist for the illustrations.

Who lives in this house?

Age range
Six to seven.

Extension age range
Eight to eleven.

What you need
Double zigzag books with four inside pages, A4 unlined paper, scissors, a curved template to outline 'flaps', paste, books about animal homes.

What to do
Gather the children together for a reading/talking session and discuss first their own homes, then the homes in which different animals live, for example, rabbits live in a burrow, birds live in a nest. This idea works particularly well if it is tackled immediately after a visit to a woodland nature trail or to a farm.

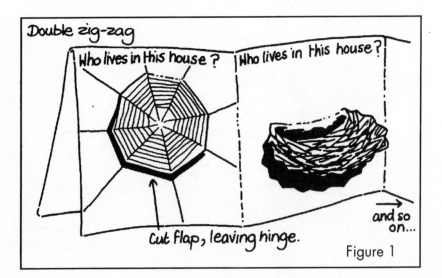

Double zig-zag

Who lives in this house? Who lives in this house?

Cut flap, leaving hinge.

and so on...

Figure 1

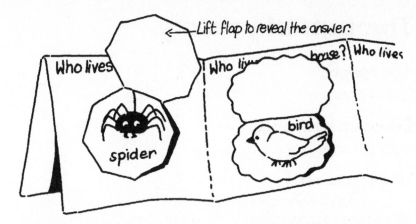

Lift flap to reveal the answer.

Who lives   Who liv   house? Who lives

spider   bird

Give out the zigzag books or encourage the children to make their own. With the fold at the top, the children should open out the zigzags and draw round the template to outline a flap on each of the four inside pages. Help them to cut open the flap, leaving a hinge at the top. (See Figure 1.) The children should paste a piece of unlined paper beneath each flap.

Above the cut-out flap, at the top of each page, the children should write out the question 'Who lives in this house?' They should then draw a different animal house on each flap. On the paper under the flap, the children should draw and write the answer to the question, for example, beneath the web flap they should draw a spider and write 'The spider lives here'.

Ask the children to print on the front cover, *Animal homes* or *Who lives in this house?* They might draw a pattern of leaves around the title on the forest homes book, or a fence and gateway pattern around the farm animals book.

Extension
Following the same pattern, older children can make animal home zigzags for the youngest children to read. The combination of opening flaps and repetitive language makes this zigzag a most attractive book for early readers.

Through the year

Age range

Five to seven.

Extension age range

Eight to eleven.

What you need

Books, pictures and poems about trees through the changing seasons, cherries, an apple, a pear, a knife, simple zigzags.

What to do

Show the children the fruit. Let them look at colour, shape and size. Let them feel the texture, smell and even taste the fruit. Cut open each fruit to find and look at the seeds or stones. Talk about the seeds growing into trees and look at pictures of fruit trees through the seasons, from blossom to fruit. (If there is an apple or cherry tree in the school grounds, even better!)

Give each child a four-page zigzag and suggest that they use a page for each season of the year. Then ask them to draw a bare apple or a cherry tree on each page. They should add pink blossom to the spring tree, green leaves for summer, bright fruit for autumn and leave the tree bare, perhaps in a snowstorm, on the winter page.

The children should use a patterned phrase to write about the tree on each page, for example, 'Look at the apple tree in spring'. On the cover they should draw a basket of apples or a bunch of cherries beneath the title, *Through the year*.

Follow-up

The children can use a similar format to make books about the hedgerows, the pond, the woods etc. at each season of the year.

They can also follow a four-page zigzag pattern to show the clothes worn at each season of the year, either by simply drawing and naming the clothes or using a simple patterned phrase, for example: 'I wear my bobble hat in winter', 'I wear my rain hat in spring' or 'I wear my sun hat in summer.'

Extension

Older children can make nature notebooks in zigzag style, again showing the changes in one environment at different seasons of the year. This book can be an ongoing activity, based on observation of the school garden or pond, for example. The children should make notes and illustrate their findings. They may start with a zigzag of about eight pages, adding more if necessary.

To add extra pages to the zigzag, simply tape the new section to the end of the previous one ensuring the joint is at the back, and fold as before. Sometimes older children can end up with a really comprehensive nature notebook of twenty-four or more pages!

Rainbows

Age range

Five to six.

What you need

A picture of a rainbow, card zigzag books cut with a curved top (as in Figure 1).

What to do

Group the children comfortably and show them a picture of a rainbow. Suggest that they now wear 'invisible poets' hats' so that they can look at the picture and think of other things which are the same shape as the rainbow, but quite different. The children may suggest a bridge, a hairband, an umbrella, a skipping rope etc.

This is an excellent way of introducing young children to the concept of 'image', that is, of using simile and metaphor (without using these terms at this stage).

Ask the children to carry their invisible poets' hats back to their tables, and write a simple image poem, copying the phrase 'A rainbow is like.......' and drawing an appropriate picture. Write out the words, for example, 'bridge', 'mountain', 'sad face', to the children's dictation. The children can copy the words so that the pages read, for example, 'A rainbow is like a sad face'.

The children should use the curved edge to colour a rainbow across the top of each page. They should put the title *A rainbow poem* on the cover and draw a pot of gold.

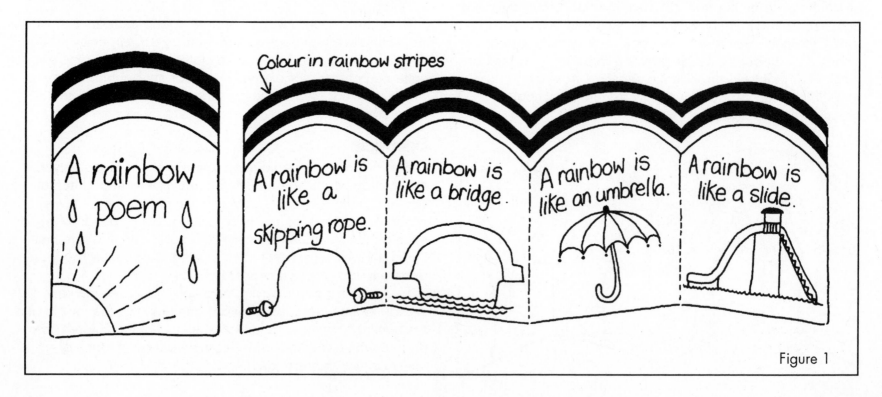

Figure 1

Growing up

Age range
Five to seven.

Extension age range
Eight to eleven.

What you need
Photographs of children of different ages, diagonally cut zigzag books (as in Figure 1).

What to do
Talk with the children about how much they have grown since they were babies. Encourage them to talk about what they can do now that they couldn't do then. Let them think of what they could do when they were one, two, three and so on.

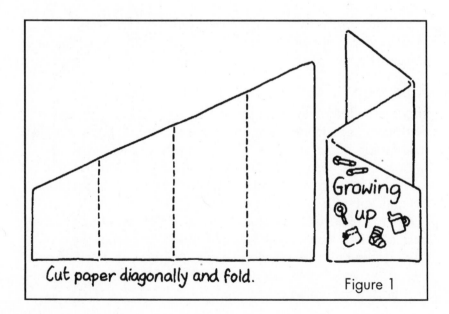

Cut paper diagonally and fold.

Figure 1

Give out the zigzags and ask the children to put the title *Growing up* on the cover. Encourage them to draw bootees, little socks, shoes, trainers and so on as a border around the title.

Explain that on page one, the children should write 'When I was one I cried/played with a rattle/sucked from a bottle'. They should draw a picture of themselves as a baby, then a toddler, taking one page at a time, for instance 'When I was two I...' and so on. Because of the shape, the zigzag book grows along with the child and page five (the back cover) should see him setting off for school.

Extension
Older children can use a similar 'growing' zigzag format to write an adventure story about climbing a mountain or going on a journey across a mountain track. This format also lends itself to non-fiction books where children can trace the growth of bulbs/beans/orange or grapefruit pips. They can use it to show the stages in building a house or to demonstrate how to make a model using LEGO bricks.

Contoured zigzags

Age range
Eight to eleven.

What you need
Fine card, scissors, scrap paper.

What to do
This activity encourages children to think in design terms and often opens up some very unusual writing possibilities. It helps them develop their book-making skills and these in turn encourage the young authors to explore a range of different and imaginative ideas for story writing.

Discuss with the children how the pages of zigzags can be shaped at the top, for example, they can be pointed like a mountain top, made jagged like a star or an icicle, cut into the shape of a roof, a church spire, a rocket and so on. (See Figure 1.)

Suggest that the children should each first design a zigzag using scrap paper. Encourage them to experiment with the contours so that the books themselves suggest a story outline, for example, a rocket shape followed by a

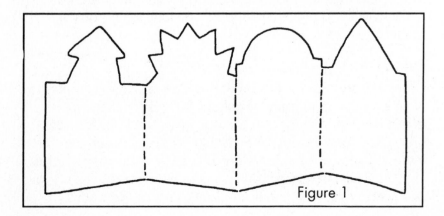

Figure 1

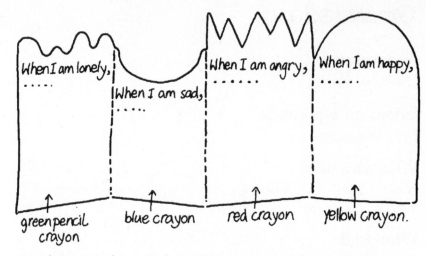

star shape might give the children an idea for a space adventure story. A wave shape followed by a rock outline might suggest an underwater story.

The children should then work on a draft story, always keeping the contour of each page in mind. When they are satisfied with their draft, ask them to cut a card zigzag to match the scrap paper outline and write out the finished story so that both words and illustrations follow the contour shape of each page.

Follow-up
Encourage the children to write zigzag books which use contoured tops to represent different emotions. For example, a spiky top could suggest 'When I am angry I could…' a smooth curved top might suggest 'When I am happy I like to…', while a down-turned top (like a sad face) might lead the children into 'When I am sad I…'.

Ask the children to design a shape signifying being brave and to write about it. Taking care not to obliterate their writing, the children should use a pencil crayon to colour the pages very lightly, using perhaps red for anger, yellow for happiness and so on.

Cinderella

Age range
Six to seven.

Extension age range
Eight to eleven.

What you need
A picture story book telling the story of Cinderella, simple zigzags, gold pen.

What to do
Help the children to fold four-page zigzags. Tell the story of Cinderella and encourage the children to work out how the story can be divided into four sections, perhaps the kitchen scene, the fairy godmother, the ballroom, Cinderella trying on her lost slipper.

Encourage the children to draw a picture and write a sentence or two on each page. They should make the cover look very grand, perhaps using a gold pen to outline a frame around the title, *The story of Cinderella*.

Follow-up
Let the children work in groups to make a book of another traditional story. Again, encourage them to look for four distinct episodes so that it can be written and illustrated in a four-page zigzag format.

The children could then build up their own library of traditional stories which could be borrowed at silent-reading time or taken home to read with their parents.

Extension
The eight-to-elevens can develop this idea using both traditional stories and myths and legends as a basis, always retelling the stories in their own words. Encourage the children to extend the basic zigzag as necessary. They might also design double zigzags with cut-out flaps so that pictures and secret messages can be hidden until the flaps are lifted.

Have you heard this one?

Age range
Eight to eleven.

What you need
Scissors, joke books, double zigzags.

What to do
This is a book much beloved by juniors, especially those who find story or poetry writing difficult, so gather the children round you and surprise them by asking if anybody knows a good joke. You could start the children off with a joke:

Q: What is the crocodile's favourite game?
A: Snap!
Q: What can run across the floor without any legs?
A: Water.

Children enjoy this kind of thing and it usually gets a good response. If the children can't remember any suitable jokes, suggest that they look in one of the books. Suggest that each child selects two jokes that have a special appeal. Explain that the children should write a joke on the first inside page of the double zigzag. Suggest best handwriting for this task so that they can take the books home to try to baffle their parents. Tell the children that they should cut out a flap on the right-hand page. On this they should write 'Lift to find out the answer', writing and/or drawing the answer underneath. In the same way, they should write out the second joke and its answer on the following two pages. (See Figure 1.)

The children may want to extend this into a group or class zigzag with a title such as *Our giant joke book* on the cover.

Figure 1

Noah's ark

Age range

Five to seven.

What you need

Zigzag books folded to make at least eight pages, animal pictures, a book about Noah's ark.

What to do

Tell the story of Noah and how he was supposed to have taken two of every animal aboard the ark. Suggest that the children choose eight kinds of creature for their book. The children should then draw two animals of the same kind on each of the eight pages, either simply naming them or writing a patterned phrase beside the drawing, for example 'Noah took two tigers'.

Suggest that the children might draw raindrops falling on the animals, making them bigger and thicker as the story progresses.

On the front cover the children should draw Noah and his wife looking up at a cloudy sky. They should put the title *Noah's ark* across the top. On the back cover they should draw the ark in a rainstorm, perhaps having the animals peeping out from the deck.

Follow-up

The children might make a long class book about Noah, each child taking a page to draw and write about a different pair of animals.

Once upon a time

Age range

Six to eight.

What you need

Several comics, stories and pictures about monsters, dragons, giants, trolls, simple zigzags.

What to do

Gather the children around you and start off as if you were about to tell a story. Begin by saying, 'Once upon a time there lived a ...' and then stop. When the children look up to see what you are going to say next, suggest that they might like to help you out. Take one or two suggestions and continue, '... there lived a dragon.' Ask the children what he looked like and where he lived. You might have a story beginning like this: 'Once upon a time there lived an ancient green dragon with warts on his nose. He lived at the top of a mountain where it was so cold that the grass was white with frost – even in summer! One day the dragon heard a voice. It was a croaky mysterious voice and it said ...'

Ask questions and offer ideas to help the children to build up a story in the style of a traditional fairy tale with perhaps a prince, three wishes and so on.

Once the bones of the story have been established, turn the children's attention to the selection of comics and suggest that they use the zigzag books to tell the fairy story in pictures and words in the style of a comic strip. Show them how to follow the convention of using speech bubbles to indicate direct speech.

On the cover page suggest that the children should write the title *Once upon a time*.

Secret messages

Age range
Eight to nine.

What you need
Scissors, double zigzags.

What to do
Sit the children in a half-circle. Explain that you intend to send an important message from one person to the next, but that somewhere along the line it will become scrambled. Try a message like this: 'Tomorrow we are going to climb Blackpool Tower.' Suggest that the message should be passed round each child changing just one thing about the sentence. For example, it might develop as follows:
• Tomorrow we are going to climb Bluepool Tower.
• Tomorrow we are going to climb a beautiful tower.

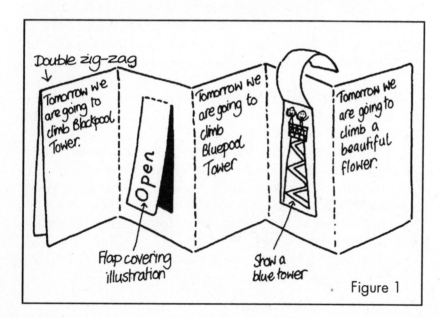

Figure 1

• Tomorrow we are going to climb a beautiful flower.
   Help the children to look for a one-word change, like black to blue, then to a word that sounds much the same, like tower to flower.

Suggest that the children work in pairs, making and writing a zigzag book of secret messages in which there is a slight change on every page so that the message on the last page bears little or no resemblance to the first. The children should cut open flaps to show pictures of the changes as the story progresses. (See Figure 1.)

On the cover the children should draw a detective, Sherlock Holmes-style, with a huge magnifying glass and the title *Secret Messages* looking out of focus beneath it.

Behind the door

Age range

Eight to eleven.

What you need

Double zigzags made from fine card, scissors, lined paper, paste, string and Blu-tack (optional).

What to do

For this zigzag, suggest that the children write an adventure story in which characters appear and disappear through gates, doors, windows or even across a drawbridge. This idea requires a double zigzag made from card, so that each episode can take place or be revealed behind an opening door.

Arrange the children in groups or pairs and encourage them to talk about their characters and places in which they might hide (under the stairs, inside a cupboard, in a haunted house, behind a castle door and so on). Their characters might find themselves imprisoned. Suggest that the children share some of their ideas with you before they begin work on their drafts, so that each author begins to build up an outline story in her imagination.

Suggest that initially the children should write up the story, page by page, on lined paper, taking care that each episode or chapter is contained on a separate sheet. Explain that they should then paste the opening part of the story on the first inside page. As the story progresses, the children should design a cut-out door, window or drawbridge as required, pasting the writing beneath it, so

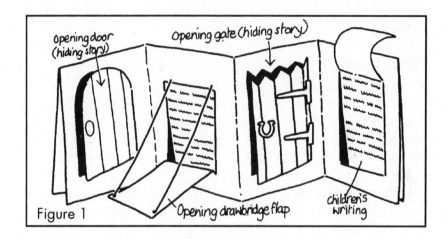

Figure 1

that the reader must open the door to read the next part of the adventure. Allow them to use string and Blu-tack if they wish to make a drawbridge. (See Figure 1.)

Secret worlds

Age range
Eight to eleven.

What you need
An apple, a pear or an orange, a knife, lined paper, paste, scissors, books and pictures about shells, butterflies, fossils, double zigzags made from card.

What to do
Show the children the fruit and suggest that it holds a secret. Of course, we all know what the inside will look like and what we will find, but nobody has ever seen inside this apple/pear/orange before. Emphasise the element of mystery. Then cut open the fruit, revealing skin, flesh, seeds or pips.

Talk to the children about the miracle of new life and share with them the wonder of the notion of a new apple tree held inside such a tiny black pip!

Encourage the children each to write about the 'secret' new life which they have found inside the fruit, describing its shape and colour, texture and size. They may also describe the taste, smell and texture of the fruit itself and say something about the tree from which it comes. This piece of writing should now be transferred to 'best' paper and, using the lightest of touch with coloured pencils, they should draw the cut-open fruit.

Explain that on the first flap the children should draw and colour a picture of the fruit that they have written about. Using pointed scissors, they should cut around the fruit-shaped flap, leaving only a 'hinge'. Ask them to paste the writing underneath, so that the reader has to open it to read about the apple's/pear's/orange's/lemon's secret. (See Figure 1.)

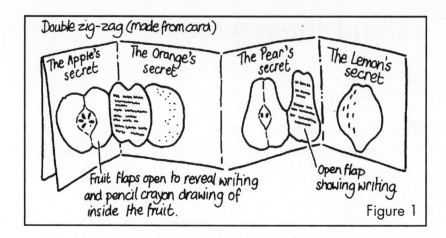

Figure 1

Now suggest to the children that they think of other natural things which hold a secret in a similar way, for example, a butterfly inside a chrysalis, a fossil inside a stone, a pearl inside an oyster shell. On each page of a double four-page zigzag the children should make an opening flap shaped like a shell, chrysalis etc., and beneath it should paste a piece of descriptive writing decorated with a butterfly, fossil and so on.

On the cover the children should write the title, *Secret worlds*. They might make a decorative border of butterflies, moths and fruit.

Follow-up
The children can make more zigzags with opening flaps. If they write about coal, for example, they could describe how it holds the secret of fire and heat.

Older children writing for their younger brothers and sisters can make story books using flaps in a similar way. The flaps should be brightly decorated with a surprise present hidden inside. The text can pose questions, for example, 'What is Grandad's surprise?', in which case the presents should be wildly inappropriate: a skateboard for grandad, a plastic spider for Great-aunt Maude etc.

The postman's bag

Age range
Five to seven.

What you need
Envelopes, paper, invitations and cards, paste, a copy of Allan and Janet Ahlberg's *The Jolly Postman*, simple zigzags made from card.

What to do
Read *The Jolly Postman* aloud to the children. Let them look at all the different kinds of invitations and cards in the book and talk about letters and cards which they themselves have received, delivered by the postman.

Let the children decide what they would like to put on a party invitation and the people (storybook characters, woodland animals, nursery rhyme characters etc.) they would like to invite. Help them to design and cut out cards to fit empty envelopes. Teach the children the important things to put on an invitation; date and time of the party, where it is to be held and so on. Let them use coloured pencils and write out and decorate their invitations.

Make up zigzags for the children and let them paste an envelope on to the first page and place the finished invitation inside. Encourage the children to write letters of thanks, make birthday cards and holiday postcards. They should write a few words about each letter or card and put it inside an envelope.

On the front cover the children should write the title, *The postman's bag*. They could then design, colour and cut out stamps to paste as a border round the title.

Books big and small

Children of all ages enjoy the challenge of the sort of book-making where they must consider not only style, but size. Where the books are tiny, they may have to alter their handwriting to accommodate the small size of the page. This often leads to careful work and detailed illustrations. Where the books are large, often the children have to share responsibility for making them. This leads to group work, consultation and decision-making among those involved.

For small books, such as diaries for tiny creatures, the children should have a range of materials and papers to choose from. Best results usually require a good quality paper so that small neat writing shows up well. Pencils need to be well-sharpened and pens of the fine-point variety.

Large books should be made from card so that they remain fairly rigid and do not 'flop' in the reader's hands. Consideration must also be given to the best means of fixing the pages of large floor books. It is often best to use a traditional sewing method, such as using blanket-stitch along the spine. You may be able to use treasury tags or have the book spiral-bound with a plastic spine. It depends, of course, on the thickness of the finished book and the amount of wear and tear it is likely to get. Large floor books may also be made in zigzag format.

The biggest book in the world

Age range
Five to eleven.

What you need
Huge sheets of paper or a roll of frieze paper folded concertina-fashion, paints and brushes, thick felt-tipped pens, rough paper for drafting, a picture-story book (for example, *Where the Wild Things Are* by Maurice Sendak), flip-chart or chalkboard.

What to do
This book-making idea can involve every class of an entire primary school!

Gather all the children in the hall and read the story aloud. Suggest that they can all help to produce the biggest book in the world, so the first thing to do will be to divide the story into as many sections as there are classes in the school. Ask the children for suggestions and use a flip-chart or chalkboard to record their ideas in story-board format. (See Figure 1.)

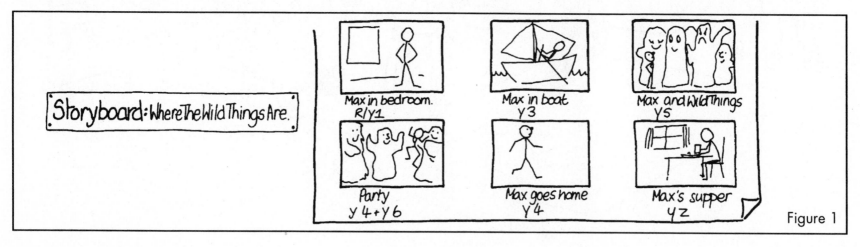

Figure 1

Back in the classrooms, work with a group of older children to produce a story-board which divides the chosen story into episodes, so that there is at least one for each class. If appropriate, suggest that they also make a draft of the written work, so that the story follows easily from episode to episode. Arrange for the children to take the story-board to each class, explaining which parts they have to illustrate and write about.

Let the different classes of children work at their own level to paint and write for their chosen sections, using thick felt-tipped pens for the writing. Children from the oldest class should co-ordinate the work, so that there is continuity.

When the book is complete, help the children to lay out the pages in order on the hall floor so that readers can 'walk through' the book, enjoying the varied interpretations which result from children at every stage of development taking part.

It may be possible to display the book in the corridor or in the assembly hall, so that parents, friends and governors of the school can enjoy reading 'the biggest book in the world'!

Follow-up

Having seen how the story-board technique works, children can be encouraged to work in groups to bring another picture-storybook to life in their own classrooms.

Gerry the giraffe

Age range

Five to seven.

What you need

Tall, narrow zigzags made from fine card (Figure 1), books and pictures about giraffes and their habitat, collage materials, scissors, paste, pencils or fine felt-tipped pens, chalkboard or personal word books.

What to do

Ask the children what they know about giraffes. Almost certainly they will first mention their long necks. Ask them to show you with their hands what would make a good shape for a book about giraffes and congratulate those who indicate something tall and narrow. (Encouraging children to choose an appropriate shape for their books is an excellent skill to develop.)

Talk with the children about the giraffe's native habitat in the grasslands of Africa: how he reaches up to find the tastiest new leaves at the top of the thorn tree; how he bends down to drink, legs splayed. Show the children pictures of the giraffe, pointing out the brown blotches on his coat and the small blunt horns on his head.

Give the children each a piece of paper which is slightly less than the upright size of the zigzag and ask them each to draw and colour a giraffe, horns touching the top of the paper, feet touching the bottom. When it is finished, ask the children to cut out the picture and explain that it will later be used collage-style on the cover of their tall zigzag book.

Talk with the children about an adventure which a giraffe might have. First give him a name, 'Gerry the giraffe', for example. Ask them questions:
• where might he go to?
• who might go with him?
• what would they look for?
• what would they find?
• would they get back home safely?

Help the children to construct their own story, giving them a set of appropriate words on the chalkboard or in their personal word books.

Allow those who can write for themselves to begin drafting the story in outline. Those who are at the stage of simple sentences can copy, for example, 'Gerry is lonely', 'Gerry looks for a friend' and so on. All the children should write a sentence or two on each page.

Then let them use the collage materials to make a collage picture for each page. Ask them to write *Gerry the Giraffe's Adventure* on the title page.

Figure 1

Diary of a spider

Age range

Six to eight.

What you need

Fine paper to make a tiny book (page size approximately 50 x 80mm) of eight pages, stapler, fine fibre-tipped pens or coloured pencils, information picture books about spiders, black embroidery cotton, needles, tiny beads or sequins, glue, a copy of *The Very Hungry Caterpillar* by Eric Carle, 50p coin.

What to do

Remind the children of the sequence of the days of the week and establish that there are seven days in the week. Show the children picture books about spiders. Talk about where spiders live, what they like to eat, how they make their webs and so on. Read the story of *The Very Hungry Caterpillar* together.

Help the children to fold the paper into zigzag format as shown in Figure 1. This will give eight sides, including the

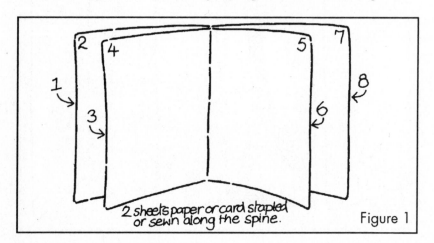

2 sheets paper or card stapled or sewn along the spine.

Figure 1

cover. If they decide to make a book stapled or sewn along the spine, they should fold over two sheets as shown, again giving eight pages, including the cover. Ask them to use the first page as a cover and give it a title such as *The Spider's Diary*. Explain that they should copy the word Monday at the top of the first inside page, Tuesday on the next and so on.

Ask the children to think about what the spider might do, eat or where it might go on each day of the week, much as Eric Carle does in *The Very Hungry Caterpillar*.

Independent writers might suggest, for example, 'Today I climbed to the top of the fence', 'Today I felt very hungry' or 'Today I started spinning a web' and so on. Those children who are not at the stage of independent writing could be allowed to put the day at the top of the page with a picture below. Either write the story to the child's dictation or use it purely as a story without words.

Let the children sew a web design using black embroidery cotton on the title page. A few sequins or beads stuck into position will look very effective. (See Figure 2.) They could use a 50p coin as a template.

scrap of fur fabric

black cotton

beads or sequins

Figure 2

Follow-up

Ask the children to write small diaries for other tiny creatures, working in the same way to a similar pattern. For example, they could choose *The Caterpillar's Diary*, *The Dragonfly's Diary* or *The Ladybird's Diary*. Encourage the children to use information and picture books to gain background information about the creature, so that the story, even if it is fictional, fits the small creature's lifestyle. Encourage the children to make tiny books in different styles, experimenting with double folds, zigzags and stitched spine books.

Grandma's balcony garden

Age range

Eight to eleven.

What you need

Card to make tall narrow books, cotton, needles with large eyes, thread, garden books and catalogues, empty seed packets, felt-tipped pens or pencil crayons, scissors, paste.

What to do

Suggest to the children that they are going to design a book which will be of practical help to people who don't have a garden, only a balcony. There may indeed be children who live in high-rise apartments or who have relatives in that situation.

The children can work in groups or pairs for this task. Suggest they make a tall book for the balcony garden project and help them to stitch the spine. Show them how to design the cover as a tower block showing only one balcony spilling over with colour. In coloured bubble writing (that is, with a double outline) they should put the title, *Grandma's Balcony Garden*. (See Figure 1.) The

Figure 1

tall format encourages work presented in list form. It may be useful for the children to measure and cut narrow strips of paper for their written work in advance, so that they can later fit it into the unfamiliar outline.

Part of this project is to encourage the children to practise and use their research skills. Explain that they will need to look at the gardening books for information about flowers and plants that can be grown on a balcony at different seasons of the year. Then ask them to find pictures of these plants to copy or cut illustrations from gardening catalogues.

Next, ask the children to work on drafts or outlines of the information which they feel would be useful, answering questions such as, 'How do we make a garden in a small space?' Using tubs or pots is the answer to this particular question, so they may go on to ask, 'What kind of soil can we use?' and 'How do we get it there?' Again, they should refer to the gardening books for the answer.

They may decide that they need to use the first two pages to offer basic advice. They should then make a draft layout, indicating the print area with pencil lines between words and illustrations, perhaps working on a 'What you need' section, followed by a 'What it costs' section (see Figure 2). This teaches the children basic layout skills and how to make the best use of space.

Now let them divide the rest of the book into spring, summer, autumn and winter pages, suggesting ideas for plants and planting, and illustrating each page, using cut-out catalogues or seed packets, collage-style. Some particularly artistic children may prefer to draw their own version of the flowers and plants, or indeed, the pages could be a mixture of both drawing and collage cut-outs.

Follow-up

The children might go on to produce books offering advice for other kinds of garden; herbs to grow in a window box,

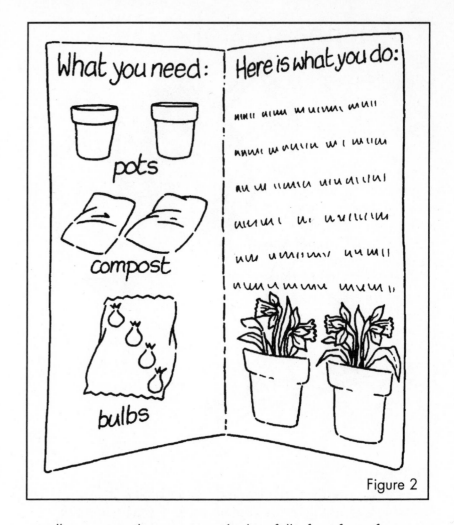

Figure 2

an all-green garden, or one which is full of perfume for a blind person to enjoy. Again, encourage the children to research their information before drafting, writing and illustrating their books.

The herb window-box book might be presented in a wide and short format, the all-green garden book on green pages and the book for blind gardeners might need to be read on to cassette tape.

The elephant's story

Age range

Five to seven.

What you need

Card cut into a landscape shape, embroidery cotton and large-eyed needles or staples and a stapler, picture books about elephants (including David McKee's book, *Elmer, the Patchwork Elephant*), chalkboard, pencils, felt-tipped pens, scraps of coloured materials for collage, scissors, glue, chalkboard.

What to do

Gather the children in the story corner and ask them to talk

staples or sewing

about the biggest animals they can think of. When the elephant is mentioned, ask about its shape, colour and what makes the elephant special and different from other animals.

Ask the children to think about the colour grey. What other creatures are grey? Can they suggest other things that are always grey? Look at a picture of an elephant and find words to describe its greyness, for example, dull, smoky, miserable. Ask the children to think of a bright magic colour which would make the elephant look quite different, for example, emerald green, turquoise, gold. The children might suggest different patterns: striped, spotted and so on.

Read *Elmer, the Patchwork Elephant* and suggest that the children write their own

elephant story. Using the chalkboard, begin with the name, perhaps Edgar the elephant. Ask the children how he was feeling (sad, cross, unhappy). So the first part of the story might read, 'Edgar was an unhappy elephant'. Why? 'He was unhappy because his coat was dull and grey.' Continue asking questions and writing the best answers on the chalkboard, so that the children can see a story growing as they watch.

Give out the card, cut to shape as 'fat' double folds. Help the children with stitching or stapling as necessary. Ask them to begin their story, copying the first sentence from the chalkboard on to the first inside page or using independent writing. Suggest that they draw a picture of a big grey elephant looking very sorry for himself.

Page 2 could show the elephant crying great fat tears, and on page 3, a magic firefly (or some such creature) could arrive, allowing Edgar to choose a different colour skin.

Encourage the children to write and draw, choosing a different colour or pattern for Edgar as the story progresses. Let them give him a new skin made from collage materials, cutting and pasting to fit their elephant outline.

On the front cover the children should put the title, *The elephant's story*, using fat bubble writing (double outline), and draw a fat, happy-looking elephant wearing a magic coat and a beaming smile.

Follow-up

Using the landscape-style format, the children could write another elephant story, for example, a version of 'How the elephant got its trunk,' from Kipling's *Just So Stories*. They could also write about other large animals such as the hippopotamus, the rhinoceros and so on. Encourage the children to write both adventure or fantasy stories as well as factual books which show the animals in their habitat.

The longest book ever

Age range
Eight to eleven.

What you need
A roll of frieze paper, drafting paper, A5 sheets of paper, glue, pens or pencils, felt-tipped pens.

What to do
Begin the activity by showing the children how to play 'Consequences'. Give out drafting paper and suggest that they make up a story in small groups. Explain that the first child should choose a character and write down the name at the top of a piece of paper (for example, 'Kate met ...'). She should then fold over the edge of the paper so that the name is hidden, and pass the paper on to the second child who adds a second name to develop the story ('... Joel in a ...'). Again, the paper is folded over and passed on with each child adding a little to the story. Finally, the last child should bring the story to a conclusion by writing '... and the consequence was ...' and finishing it appropriately. The first child could then open out the paper and read out the whole story ('Kate met Joel in a railway station. She said, "Shall

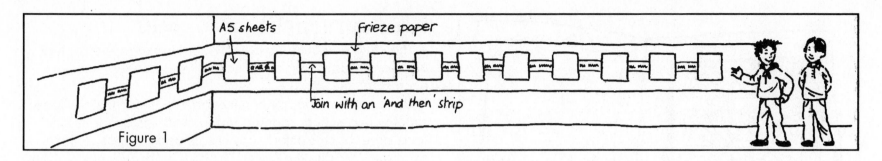

A5 sheets   Frieze paper

Join with an 'And then' strip

Figure 1

we go and see the gorillas first?" He said, "My aunty is a lollipop lady." And the consequence was that they both got very wet'). The length of the story will depend on the size of the group.

Using this principle, all the children in the class could help to write 'the longest story ever'. Pin the roll of frieze paper on to the classroom wall at a height convenient to the children, and make A5 sheets available to everybody. (See Figure 1.) Choose a child who can write well to start the story off. Ask her to invent two characters, and put them in a setting to begin the adventure. Explain that she should not take up more than one A5 page. At an interesting point in the story, suggest that she writes 'And then' and pastes her sheet of paper on to the left-hand edge of the frieze-paper roll.

The story should then be continued by a second writer. Each child should contribute one A5 sheet, always finishing at an exciting point which the next writer has to solve. This task may well take the best part of a week, as only one writer is working on it at any one time. (Meanwhile, the rest of the class may be working on other projects.) Encourage the children to illustrate their work as the story takes shape. Again, choose an accomplished writer to complete the story, his contribution beginning 'And the consequence was...'.   This writing project causes a great deal of fun; children from other classes often come in to read the next exciting instalment!

Down the village street

Age range

Six to seven.

What you need

A large double zigzag made from card (folded landscape so that each section measures at least 300 x 200mm), pens or pencils, clear adhesive film, felt-tipped pens, paper, glue or adhesive tape, scissors, clipboards.

What to do

This idea works well in connection with a topic on the local environment. Take the children on a visit to the local shopping centre or village street. Ensure that each child has a clipboard, paper and a pencil.

Suggest that the children note down, either in words or pictures, each kind of shop they see. Ask the children to work in groups and draw and name some of the things they see in the shop windows. Explain that they should copy down the names of the shops and show some of the labels or advertising in the windows.

Back in the classroom, unfold the long zigzag and explain that the children are going to work together to make a book about the village street (or shopping centre). The first section will be the cover and will show a title such

Cut out shop window and back with clear film.

Figure 1

as *Down the Village Street* or *Our Visit to the Shopping Centre*. Let the children decide on which shop each separate group is going to work. Show the children how the inside of the zigzag will become the shop windows. Give the children sheets of paper, and let them draw, colour and cut out separate items which will later be pasted into the window space. For example, the toyshop might have teddy bears, dolls, computer games and so forth, while the greengrocer might have apples, oranges, peppers, fruit juice and suchlike in his window.

Help the children to draw and cut out 'windows' on the outside part of the zigzag, leaving enough space for them to write below. Glue or tape clear film behind to create a window pane effect, and let the children paste their items into their own shop window a group at a time. (See Figure 1.)

They might also want to show the shop doorway and perhaps draw, cut out and paste a picture of the owner standing outside his shop. (See Figure 2.)

Follow-up

• The children could make individual zigzags with written work and illustrations to tell something about what makes each stop special.

• Use a pack of Happy Family cards to introduce a village street with a similar format. Suggest that the children build up a street of characters with words and pictures of, for example, 'Mr Bun the Baker', 'Miss Bun the Baker's daughter' and so on, inventing new shops and new characters as they go along. Independent writers can suggest what might happen to the various shops and the people who work there at special times of the year (for example, the snowstorm, or Christmas in the village or the day the sweet shop caught fire). Books could then be made and written on an individual or a group basis.

• Make long class books about train journeys, using the zigzag format, perhaps after a journey along the local line. Suggest that the children consult a map beforehand, listing the stations along the way. They can draw and write about each place, suggesting interesting things travellers should look out for.

Figure 2

Our favourite toys

Age range
Five to seven.

Extension age range
Eight to eleven.

What you need
Large sheets of card (at least A2 in size), felt-tipped pens or paints and brushes, paper, pens or pencils, scissors, paste, picture story books, coloured string, hole puncher, adhesive hole reinforcements, letter stencils.

What to do
Very young children enjoy lying on the floor looking through a really big book, especially if they themselves have helped to make it. Suggest that the children each paint or draw a picture of their own favourite toy. Give the children each a sheet of paper almost as big as a page of the floor book and ask them to make their picture fill the paper portrait format, head touching the top, feet touching the bottom. Then ask them to cut their pictures out, waiting for them to dry first if they have used paints. Help them to paste the cut-outs on to a page of the floor book, leaving room underneath to label the painting, for example, 'My best teddy. His name is Herbert', and to add their name. Use a felt-tipped pen to make a border for each page. Punch several holes at the top of each page, stick on reinforcements and use string to tie the book together, so that the pages flip over. (See Figure 1.)

Stencil the title, *Our Favourite Toys* on the cover and encourage one child to fill in the letters carefully with felt-tipped pen. Put the name of the class beneath the title and add some cut-out paintings of toys as decoration.

Figure 1

Follow-up
Use the same method to make floor books about almost any class topic; *Our Pets, Our Favourite Foods, Hot and Cold, Floating and Sinking* and so on.

Extension
The large floor book is an ideal assignment on which a group of top juniors can work together to produce a book for the youngest children in the school to read and enjoy.

Before making a start, the writers should do some research. Encourage them to look at a few early readers to see how much text goes on each page, to look at the short sentences, to note the kind of words used and so on. Their attention should also be drawn to the way in which illustrations are used to help tell the story.

The group should decide on the characters (not more than three). Dragons and dinosaurs are favourites for this age group rather than furry bunnies. Next they should decide on a simple storyline, and prepare it on a storyboard. Help them to make decisions about size and shape of the finished book, number of pages and so on. At this stage, they may need your editorial input to make sure that their ideas will work. The group must work co-operatively, deciding on responsibility for the writing and handwriting (not necessarily undertaken by the same person), bookmaking and artwork.

When the book is completed, the group should take it into the infant class, gather the children together in the story corner and read the story and show the pictures to their intended audience. The floor book will then become a welcome addition to the infant library.

Tom Thumb's adventures

Age range
Eight to eleven.

You will need
Drafting paper, cartridge paper, scissors, cotton and needles, fine felt-tipped pens, pens, a picture story of *Tom Thumb* or *Mrs Pepperpot*, chalkboard.

What to do
Ask the children to look at the size of their thumbs and think of some advantages and disadvantages of being so small. On the chalkboard make lists of advantages and disadvantages, then suggest that the children make their own lists on drafting paper, taking two ideas from the chalkboard and adding two of their own. Ask them to think about how they would get around, what they might eat, and how they would feel if they were Tom Thumb-size.

Read either *Tom Thumb* or a *Mrs Pepperpot* adventure aloud and suggest that the children draft out a few possible scenarios for a story, centring on the idea that they have been turned into a miniature version of themselves. Ask them to consider questions such as:
• What will your family say?
• How will you get home from school?

Once the stories have been drafted (they should not be too long), each child should use cartridge paper to make a tiny book in which to write their story of life as a very small person. Help them to work out how many pages they will need and how best to stitch the spine. Ideally, every book will look different, although all should be as small as they can manage, while still being legible.

Through an artist's eyes

Age range
Eight to eleven.

What you need
A2 card, reproductions of famous works of art (Van Gogh, Monet etc.), paints and brushes, cartridge paper, bonding material, pens, drafting paper, strong adhesive tape, thick black pens, books about the lives of famous artists.

What to do
A large format zigzag is an excellent method of displaying children's work developed from studying the work of famous artists. Prepare an A2 card zigzag of ten or twelve pages, edged with strong adhesive tape so that it will stand upright.

Encourage the children to look closely at a reproduction of a famous painting, for example, Van Gogh's *A Cornfield with Cypresses*. Encourage the children to talk about the way the artist has used paint in thick harsh strokes (nothing delicate about this painting). Discuss with them the colours, the bold shapes, the feeling of oppression in the clouds and so on. Talk about how Van Gogh gives the impression of movement in the trees, corn and the clouds.

Ask the children to imagine how they would feel if they were standing alone just outside the picture – cold, lonely, scared perhaps? What would be happening to their hair and their clothes in such weather? What sounds might they hear? Suggest that the children note down some of these ideas on their drafting sheets.

The children should then work in pairs, first choosing a picture from which to work, asking and answering questions as above, making a draft list of feelings, sounds, colours and so on.

Then explain that one of the pair should paint a copy of the picture, using a similar technique to that used by the artist, and that the other child should write a poem or diary piece about standing just outside the frame, looking in on the scene which the artist has painted, using vocabulary from the draft list. Later, the children may wish to change roles.

When the painting is dry and the piece of writing has been copied out carefully, ask the children to mount the

Cut out letters and paste on.

Sunflowers painted and cut out, then pasted on to make a border.

work inside the zigzag book, so that the picture and the written work are on facing pages. Get them to make frames for both pictures and writing using a strong black line.

Encourage other pairs of children to work in a similar way to depict other paintings by the same artist until the book is almost complete, then ask them to add a biography on the last page.

Get them to design an appropriate cover, for example a border of sunflowers for a book about Van Gogh, or water lilies for Monet. Help them to make a title for the book by cutting out letter shapes and sticking them on to read: *Through an Artist's Eyes*.

Alice grows up

Age range
Eight to eleven.

What you need
Cartridge paper, scissors, needle and cotton, a copy of *Alice through the Looking Glass*, drafting paper.

What to do
Read the chapter from *Alice through the Looking Glass* in which she drinks from the 'Drink me' glass and grows taller and taller. Suggest that the children write their own story based on this idea, where they eat a burger, drink a Coke

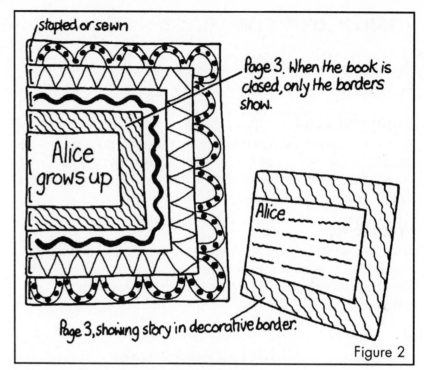

Page 3. When the book is closed, only the borders show.

Page 3, showing story in decorative border.

Figure 2

or suck on a toffee which makes them grow to the size of a giant. Ask them to draft the story in such a way that each section is longer than the one before.

Suggest that they each make a 'growing' book for their 'growing' story and discuss various ways of constructing it. Demonstrate to the children the methods illustrated in Figure 1 which shows a multi-page book with each page cut wider than the one before and a card book with each page bigger all round than the previous one. Encourage the children to think up their own ideas as well.

When they have made their books, get the children to write their stories and illustrate each page. Explain that if they use one of the books shown in Figure 2, they should write each part inside a coloured frame, so that before the book is opened only the frames show.

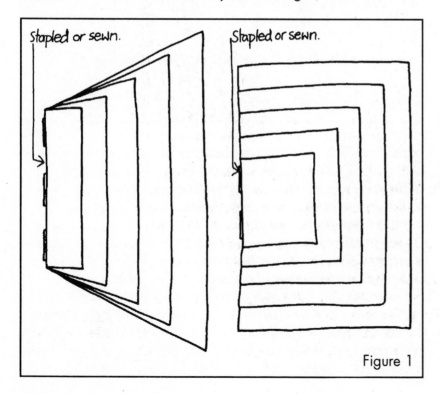

Figure 1

Inside the castle

Age range

Eight to eleven.

What you need

Ten sheets of A3 card, tape, scissors, rulers, pens or pencils, a plan of a medieval castle, chalkboard, felt-tipped pens, glue, unlined paper, books about King Arthur and the Knights of the Round Table.

What to do

This idea works best after a visit to a castle, but it could be tackled successfully from pictures and a discussion. Look at the books together and discuss with the children the different parts of the castle; the great hall, sleeping

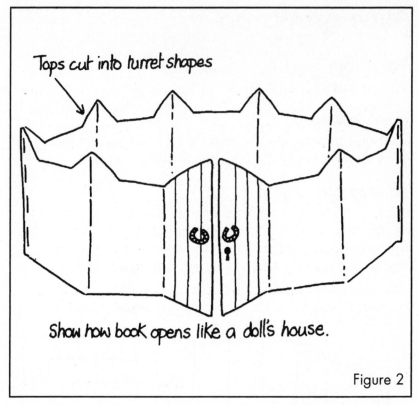

Tops cut into turret shapes

Show how book opens like a doll's house.

Figure 2

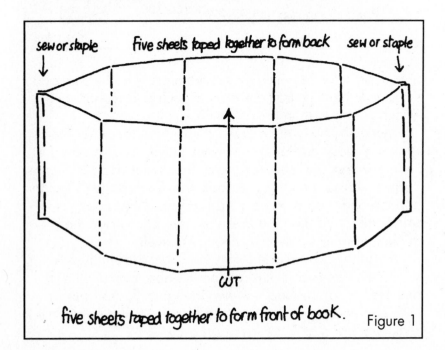

sew or staple   five sheets taped together to form back   sew or staple

CUT

five sheets taped together to form front of book.

Figure 1

accommodation, kitchens etc. Plan a book together on the chalkboard, showing the children how the card can be taped together with five sheets at the back, portrait style, and five at the front, with the book opening down the middle sheet (the castle door), as in Figure 1.

Get some of the children to design and cut out the turrets, matching front to back, and others to work on what will become the interiors, using sheets of unlined paper.

In outline, the book will now consist of five turreted sections with a doorway in the middle. Help the children to cut down the exact middle of the shaped doorway and the central turret. This is where the book will open, rather like an old-fashioned doll's house. (See Figure 2.)

Ask some of the children to decorate the outside part of the book, adding slit windows, stones on the wall, slated turrets etc. Explain that they should make the door look wood-panelled with heavy latches.

Get those who have been working on the interior to paste on the grand hall scene, with King Arthur, his knights and their ladies round a table, and a huge fire glowing in the fireplace. Open out the castle book and paste in bedroom and kitchen interiors with cooks and servants, children, soldiers, jesters and so on. (Suggest that the children research the details of life in medieval times.)

Follow-up

Encourage the children to write stories about King Arthur and his Knights. Collect these in another book heavily embellished with illuminated script, using gold pen around the edges. The two books should be used in conjunction, the first as a display model, the second as a class story book.

Groups of children might follow this task by using the opening-out book method to illuminate other topics in history or science, for example, the inside of the *Titanic*, an opening-out version of a space craft, a version which shows the interior of a busy hospital, or how the plumbing works at home!

Information books

This kind of book encourages children to share ideas and enthusiasms with each another. It also encourages them to develop and practise the skills of research and can teach them to make their writing economical and precise.

The information book may vary from a single sheet pamphlet to a book several chapters long. What the children should be encouraged to think about, before they set about the task, is which format best suits the needs of both reader and writer. For example, a single sheet with diagrams and a short text would be ideal for describing the rules of a playground game, but quite inadequate to explain the complexities of caring for a hamster/kitten/rabbit. Another consideration is whether the information is likely to be of lasting interest, in which case a stapled or bound book might be needed. For simple information about the times and dates of the school fair or Christmas concert a single sheet would be quite adequate.

If the children are making an information book they will need good quality paper, pens or pencils, felt-tipped pens, staples and a stapler or needle and cotton. If it is to be a single sheet, it should be at least A4 and, as before, pens, pencils and felt-tipped pens will be required.

It is also important to decide with the children, before they begin, whether these books are to be individual tasks or worked on as a group or class project.

Autumn leaf collections

Age range
Five to seven.

What you need
Plastic bags for the leaf collection, autumn leaves, glue or clear adhesive film, double-fold books stapled on the spine, pencils, felt-tipped pens or coloured pencils, books on tree and leaf recognition, chalkboard.

What to do
In the autumn term, arrange a visit to a woodland nature trail or use the school grounds or local park. Take a book about tree recognition which shows the outline of trees in winter. Give every child a plastic bag and tell them to choose only leaves which have fallen on the ground. Suggest that they collect a specified number, perhaps ten, and emphasise that they should look for as many different shapes of leaf as possible. Explain that it is no use having ten specimens of beech and none of horse chestnut.

Ask the children to look at the shape of the trees from which the leaves have come. Help them to identify the most common trees and show the children how to use the tree recognition book for those that are less familiar. Back in the classroom, ask the children to lay out their leaf collection on a table. Ask each child to choose just one of each variety to keep.

Help them to identify them if necessary and draw and label the basic outlines on the chalkboard.

Give the children each a double-fold book and ask them to decorate the cover before working on the inside pages as it is difficult to keep the book flat after the leaves have been pasted into it. The children should title the book, *My Autumn Leaf Collection*, add their name, then draw and

When we went to the park I found a beech leaf.
It was brown and dry.

Sticky back plastic holding fallen leaf in place.

Drawing of beech tree.

colour a border of leaves in autumn colours.

Explain that the children should take a new page for each new leaf. Help them to paste the leaves into place or laminate the pages with clear adhesive film, then label them correctly. Ask them to draw the shape of the tree from which it comes beside the leaf. Children who can write independently can write a few sentences about where the leaves were found, the date of the trip to the woodland trail, what the weather was like, and so forth.

Follow-up

In the summer the children can make a similar book about wild flowers. However, they should only be allowed to pick and press those which are common (daisies, buttercups etc.). They can draw pictures of rarer flowers, either from direct observation or from studying illustrations in reference books. Encourage the children to sort their flowers into groups by looking at the petals, for example, compiling a page of flowers with red petals, a page of flowers with four petals each and so on.

Encourage the children to make more books of collections, for example a collection of bark rubbings using wax crayons. These can be pasted into a book, labelled and written about. If they collect buttons or coins, again rubbings can be used.

Our visit to the museum

Age range
Five to seven.

Extension age range
Eight to eleven.

What you need
For the younger children: A2 card, paper, paste, scissors; for the older children: paper, staples and a stapler or needles and cotton; for all age ranges: felt-tipped pens, pens or pencils, brochures about the museum, clipboards.

What to do
Prepare the children for the museum visit by showing them the brochures, asking them to suggest the things that they most want to see, and giving guidelines for how to use the clipboards for note-taking and sketching. (Some museums

give out ready-made questionnaires, so it is worthwhile showing the children how to concentrate on simple, one word answers. You don't want them to spend all their time on the questionnaire, and not enough on looking at the interesting things on display!)

It may also be helpful to suggest that each group has one particular aspect to work on, so that the class gets some overall feedback from the visit.

Once back in the classroom, help the children to use their notes and sketches to draw and label things of interest, one group concentrating, for example, on dinosaurs, another on local history and so on. Let each group prepare a page on their own particular topic, making a collage of written and illustrated work. Ask one group to work on the cover with the title, *Our Visit to the Museum*, and adding the class name or number. Independent writers can add some information about how they travelled to the museum, how much it cost, where the toilets were, which exhibits were of greatest interest, and so on. Explain that this sort of information will make it useful as a guide book (Figure 1).

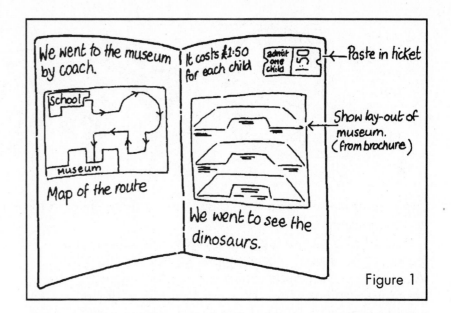

Figure 1

When all the pages are ready, gather them together and either staple or sew them along the spine. Suggest that the children show and read the finished book to the other classes in assembly. They can answer questions about the visit and explain the process of making and writing the book to the rest of the school.

Extension

Older children could follow the same basic process, taking notes and making sketches on the day of the visit. Back in the classroom, however, they could be asked to use reference books to find out more about exhibits which are of particular interest, adding this information to their written work. Let them use diagrams, drawings and photographs cut from the brochures to add detail and interest.

Encourage the children to make books to their own design, working out not only how to show their own work to best advantage, but ensuring that their readers learn something about what the museum offers. They might also

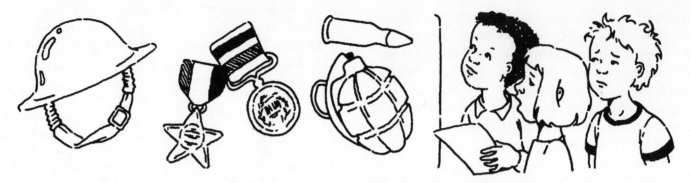

make pamphlets and posters to encourage other children to visit the museum.

As part of a history topic, the children could set up a museum-type display, for example, on the Second World War. This could include ration cards, identity cards, photographs, maps and drawings. Stress that all the exhibits should be labelled and dated. Encourage the children to make a pamphlet, like the museum brochure, and perhaps record a tape to go with their display. They could also make posters advertising their museum to display around the school.

To complete the class museum, they might like to act as guides to answer visitors' questions about the exhibits.

Magic paintings

Age range
Five to seven.

Extension age range
Eight to eleven.

What you need
A simple fold pamphlet made from sugar paper for each child, a white wax crayon, thin water-colour paint, brushes, pencils, chalkboard.

What to do
With the children, work through the steps of making a wax-resist painting over a white wax crayon drawing. Suggest to the children that they make a book which will show other people how to make these 'magic' paintings.

Give out the pamphlets and ask the children to write the title *Make Magic Paintings!* near the top of the cover. Ask the children to help you write up a list of 'What you need' on the chalkboard, then get them to copy the list of materials underneath the title. This should read: 'You will need a sheet of sugar paper, a white wax crayon, thin water-colour paint and a brush.'

On the first page, ask them to write out 'Here is what you do', followed by '1. Draw a picture on white paper with a white crayon.' Ask them to illustrate this with a drawing in white crayon. (It won't show up properly, of course.)

On the next page let them write out the second step: '2. Brush over the white drawing with thin paint. It is magic!' To illustrate this the children should draw another picture in white crayon and brush with thin brightly-coloured paint as described, so that the picture shows up.

On the last page, ask the children to draw another picture in white wax crayon. Explain that this time it will be left for the reader to find out what it is. Ask the children to write: '3. Can you guess what this picture is? Brush over it with thin paint to find out.'

Follow-up

The children could write more easy-to-follow pamphlets describing how to make bark rubbings, a collage picture or a leaf print. They will have to try out these activities for themselves first, then list the things they need. Next they should work out the steps and write these out as concisely as possible, adding drawings or partly finished work to show each stage in the process.

Extension

Older children could be asked to make booklets to show a more complicated artwork process. This should be a technique which they themselves have tried out first, and they should carefully list the things they need. For example, they could explain how to make comb paintings, mobiles, scraper board pictures and so on. Encourage them to add examples of their own partly-done and finished work and say how the technique might be adapted to make cards or Christmas decorations etc.

The children could build up a library of booklets and pamphlets on various artwork techniques which other classes might wish to borrow. Display enlarged examples of each technique above the 'How to' books.

No doubt they would be very thrilled to see ideas taken from their information books adapted and put on display in classrooms around the school.

Grandma's recipes

Age range
Eight to eleven.

What you need
Good quality paper or sheets of A5 card, pens and pencils, clear adhesive film, hole punch, thick card, scissors, felt-tipped pens, treasury tags, various recipes and old-fashioned recipe books, a cooker and ingredients/utensils (optional).

What to do
Ask the children to collect one or two favourite recipes from a grandparent or an elderly neighbour. Read them through together to see if they include anything that is difficult to acquire today. If so, it might be possible to suggest substitutes.

If there are cooking facilities in school, try out some of the recipes with the children (often parents will be able to help with this), simplifying the method if necessary. Let the children sample the results, voting for those they like best.

Ask the children to work in groups to produce either a recipe book or a set of recipe cards. Stress that each recipe should be written out neatly, with the ingredients listed and the method shown in clear steps. The children might like to illustrate the recipe or make a decorative border around it, for example, putting apples and blackberries round a recipe for jam, or lemons bordering a pancake recipe.

Encourage the children to add a sentence or two to personalise each recipe. For recipes which have a strong regional bias, the children could describe the place from which they originated. Alternatively they might write something about the relative or neighbour who made the contribution, especially if there is an anecdote to go with it.

Get the children to decide on the style of book they want to make. For example, they could select a conventional

Figure 1

Figure 2

Insert recipe card into pocket

Put a ribbon bow to look like an apron pocket.

Fold card up and tape to back to form a pocket.

Figure 3

Fix 4 or more cards together using treasury tags. Because they are flexible the cards can be turned over and used one by one.

format, either zigzag or single-fold stapled at the spine, or they might wish to make a book in the shape of a jam pot or an apple as in Figure 1. Ask the children to decorate the cover and add the title, *Grandma's Recipes*. To complete the book, they should seal the cover with clear adhesive film, so that the books can be used in the kitchen and wiped clean, if necessary.

If the children choose to make a set of recipe cards, let them use A5 card. Help them to cover each card with clear film, then punch holes at the top edge. Use treasury tags to tie several cards together, so that they can be turned over and used separately (see Figure 2). Finally, ask them to make a pocket in which to keep the recipe card set, using fairly thick card folded to make a pocket as shown in Figure 3. The set of recipe cards should fit neatly into it.

Follow-up

The children could collect simple DIY ideas which might be of help around the house and present them in a similar way. For example, they could write instructions for making a 'greenhouse' from a plastic bag, a garden pot and an elastic band, or a bird box from an empty milk carton, then present these ideas in a pocket format.

Going on school camp

Age range

Ten to eleven.

What you need

Maps, brochure from the camp site, photographs and diaries from previous successful camps, photo corners, paste, scissors, felt-tipped pens, pens, coloured pencils, good quality paper, staples and stapler or needle and cotton, chalkboard, photocopier, road maps, bus and rail timetables.

What to do

As a follow-up to a school camping trip, ask the children to write 'holiday brochures' for children who have not attended camp before. Let them choose whether the books are to be individual efforts or written as a group.

Ask the children to make a list of things they would like to have known about or questions to which they would have liked an answer before they set off, for example:
• How do you get your clothes dried if you get wet?
• What kind of homework do they give you?
• Is there anything extra you wish you had had with you?
• What happens if you wake up with a stomach ache in the middle of the night?

Even if the children have elected to write individual brochures, encourage them to work in groups at the drafting stage. Each group should offer its own perspective on the camp. For example, one group might choose to answer factual questions (they might also do some research to find out what the prospective campers most want to know), while others might choose to write about what being on camp feels like.

Books might be divided into the following sections:

- Things you need;
- Getting there;
- Settling in;
- Trips and visits;
- Things that happened last year;
- Highlights (midnight feasts, the last night barbeque);
- The camp diary;
- Pen portraits of the teachers;
- Setting off for home;
- Your questions answered.

Allow the children to use a combination of photocopied material (such as the list of things to take) alongside their own personal suggestions, for example, 'It's a good idea to take a plastic bag for your dirty washing'. Encourage them to use road maps, rail timetables, extracts from their own

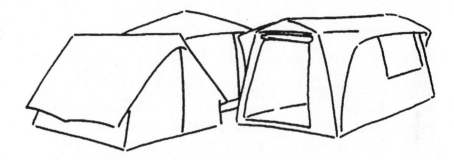

camp diaries, stories and poems, as well as photographs (attached with photo corners) and drawings.

Point out that they should include factual information, for example, a plan of the campsite showing where to find the toilets, the first aid tent or the dining marquee, as well as more personal stories of everyday life on camp: 'The funniest thing that happened last year' or 'The day Marcus fell out of a tree' or 'The day Mr Davies got lost in the forest'. Explain that the finished books should make the school camp sound interesting, exciting and a lot of fun.

Follow-up

Encourage the children to write a pamphlet about other places of interest, designed to be read by children from another school or by pupils younger than themselves. Give them similar guidelines to those suggested above, and let them use brochures, maps, photographs and drawings, their own poems, creative writing and stories resulting from the visit. They should research the history of the place, identify buildings of interest, and point out trees, birds and flowers to look out for.

Encourage the children to design their books to complement the content, for example, a forest scene cut zigzag fashion around tree shapes or a church shape with an opening door as its cover (see Figure 1).

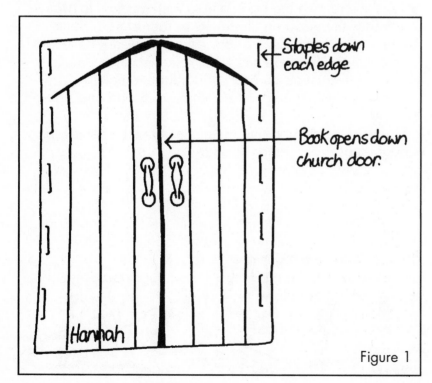

Staples down each edge

Book opens down church door.

Hannah

Figure 1

How to make a touch box

Age range
Eight to eleven.

What you need
A double-fold book (eight pages) for each child, pens and pencils, felt-tipped pens, a tea towel or silk scarf, a cardboard box with a lid (at least as big as a shoe box), scissors, a pair of old socks, adhesive tape, a miscellaneous collection of things to feel (an orange, a tennis ball, a sponge, a shell, a fir cone and so on).

What to do
Wrap one of the collection of objects in the tea towel or scarf, then ask the children to shut their eyes and guess what is under the cloth just by touch. Is this an easy task? Work out with the children what they would need to make a 'touch box' where things can be hidden and not seen, but touched.

Show the children the lidded box and tell them that they are going to help you to make it a 'touch box'. Suggest that in order to keep the objects secret, they cut two holes in the side of the box (about 120mm diameter). Help them to cut the toe ends off the old socks and tape them inside the holes. Hide a shell, orange or fir cone in the box and let the children take turns to put their hands into the box through the socks and guess by touch what the object is.

Now suggest that the children work together to write out the instructions to make the touch box, beginning with a list of 'What you need'. When the children have drafted their list of instructions and numbered it, give out the books and suggest that they work out how best to make a book with drawings and diagrams explaining how to make a touch box.

Ask them to give the book a title, such as *How to Make a Touch Box*, then add an illustrated border of fruit, shells, stones and so forth. On the first inside page, ask them to write out the 'What you need' list, followed by a simple numbered instruction on each page, for example:
1. Draw two circles about 120mm diameter on one side of the box.
2. Use scissors to cut round the circles to make holes big enough to put your hands through.

Let them continue in this way until the book is completed, perhaps putting a question and a drawing on the last page, for example, 'Can you guess what *this* is just by touch?'

Follow-up

Use these instructions to make other kinds of 'How to' book. Children should be encouraged to search among simple science books which may suggest ways of making, for example, a kaleidoscope, an anemometer or a tin-can telephone. Encourage them to collect the things needed, and to try it out for themselves, working out the steps involved, before making a book outlining the process. They should then add drawings and diagrams, as required. This kind of writing encourages children not only to think in a logical way, but also to write down their thoughts clearly and precisely so that someone reading the book would be able to follow the instructions.

Ten things to do when you have chickenpox

Age range
Eight to eleven.

What you need
A class book, felt-tipped pens, pens and pencils, scissors, glue, books of activities which can be adapted for children who are ill in bed.

What to do
This topic works well when there is a chickenpox epidemic and children are off school feeling groggy, but not really ill. Instead of the usual 'Get well' card, those who are left in class could make a big book of ideas to keep children occupied while they are ill in bed. This book can be loaned out to one child after another.

Discuss with the children how they felt when they had to stay at home in bed. (Bored? Wanting attention all the time? Needing things to do that don't take too much time or thought?)

Get the children to think of things that would not be suitable for playing with in bed, for example, felt-tipped pens, paints, water. Then ask for suggestions of things that they could use safely – coloured pencils, books, jigsaws.

Ask them to work in groups, with each group thinking up one suitable activity for someone who is ill in bed and then drafting it out. Then bring the class back together and discuss which ideas would work best.

Explain that each group will be responsible for completing one page of the class book, covering a single activity from 'What you need' to the outcome in such a way that a child could easily follow the instructions.

As time goes on, the book can be added to – perhaps one of those at home in bed can suggest a new idea to be put into the book until the *Ten Things to Do When You Have Chickenpox* becomes *Twenty-four Things!*

Here are ten ideas to start the book off:
• a game of patience explained;
• making and dressing paper dolls;
• a crossword puzzle (made up by the children);
• learning a magic trick;
• making finger puppets;
• making and writing a book;
• keeping a diary;
• making clothes-peg dolls;
• inventing a treasure island (or other) board game;
• making up a secret code (with its own key).

The children will have many more ideas, including computer games and books. Encourage them to think of activities where they must take an active part, the only rule being that it mustn't be too messy!

Put the finished pages into a loose-leaf book, perhaps with plastic pockets to hold pieces of a jigsaw which the children have made. This should be a 'growing' book, with different children borrowing it and adding to the contents as the chickenpox season comes and goes.

The children might enjoy designing a cover with an all-over red spot pattern.

How to look after your hamster

Age range
Seven to eleven.

What you need
Information books about hamsters, double-fold or zigzag books for each child, pens or pencils, felt-tipped pens or coloured pencils.

What to do
If the class has a hamster as a pet, the children will be very familiar with them and with their routine. Where there isn't one in the school, try to arrange for someone to bring in a pet hamster and talk about it to the children. Let the children familiarise themselves with the animal, watching how it feeds and moves, listening to any noises it makes and touching it, perhaps.

Writing a book about pet care requires considerable research on the part of the children, so help them to make up a list of things they need to know or find out about. Organise the class into groups and give each one responsibility for finding out about a particular area, for example choosing your hamster, feeding, handling, general care and so on.

Encourage the children to draft out and share their findings, then write individual books with facts, drawings and diagrams. They might also write poems and stories about the hamster. Those who own hamsters could add photographs of their own pets to the 'How to' book.

Follow-up
• The children could also make and write books about caring for kittens or rabbits. Encourage those who are, for example, pigeon fanciers or whose dads race greyhounds or who live on a farm, to write books about caring for the animals they know most about.
• Where there is a new baby in the home, children can be encouraged to make a book about how they help mum and dad to look after the new sister or brother. Again, encourage research, asking and answering questions. The finished book should include drawings, photographs, poems and stories.
• Let the children tackle fantasy subjects, such as *How to Look After Your Dragon* or *How to Look After Your Stegosaurus*, basing the books on the structure they used for hamsters and rabbits.

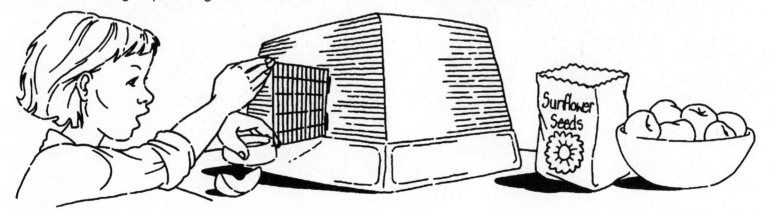

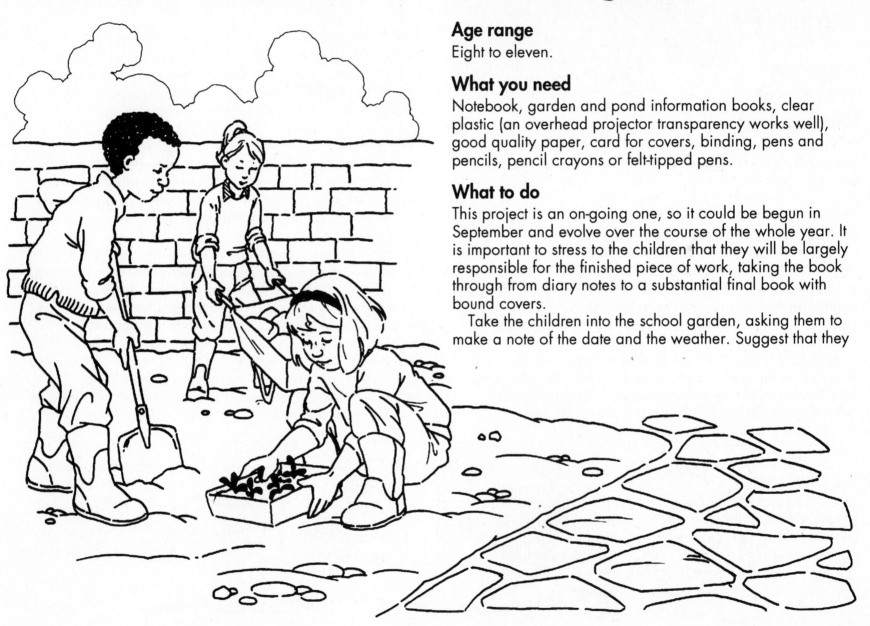

The school garden

Age range

Eight to eleven.

What you need

Notebook, garden and pond information books, clear plastic (an overhead projector transparency works well), good quality paper, card for covers, binding, pens and pencils, pencil crayons or felt-tipped pens.

What to do

This project is an on-going one, so it could be begun in September and evolve over the course of the whole year. It is important to stress to the children that they will be largely responsible for the finished piece of work, taking the book through from diary notes to a substantial final book with bound covers.

Take the children into the school garden, asking them to make a note of the date and the weather. Suggest that they

look for and make a note of any insects, flowers, fallen leaves or pond life they see. Get them to make quick sketches where necessary, showing the shapes and colours of flower petals and leaves, sizes and patterns of insects and so on.

Repeat this on a regular basis, following the same routine each time. Over the year the children will notice changes taking place. Encourage them to note down all they see and the sounds they can hear. When they work in the garden, digging, planting or weeding, they should note this too.

Back in the classroom, provide the children with garden and pond round-the-year guides for background information. Once a month allow them to write up their rough notes into draft form, then transfer their work into 'best' with diagrams, photographs, drawings and pressed leaves where appropriate. Ask them to research seasonal sayings to put at the top of each month's work, for example, 'If Candlemas be fine and clear, there'll be two winters in that year'. (Candlemas is on 2nd February.)

Make covers for the books from strong card and encourage the children to decorate them. For example, they could design a wax resist pattern with flowers and leaves, washed over with green for a garden book, while for a pond book, they could make fish and weed patterns washed with blue, perhaps covered by the OHP transparency to give a water effect.

Picture dictionary

Age range
Five to seven.

Extension age range
Eight to eleven.

What you need
Alphabet books, a wall dictionary, animal books, cartridge paper to make a long book (300 x 100mm approximately), hole punch, hole reinforcements, treasury tags, pencils, felt-tipped pens, chalkboard.

What to do
Help the children to make a long narrow book of 26 pages. Each page should have a ruled line 180mm long on which the children will write out their descriptions. The end of the page will be folded back, as shown in Figure 1, to hide a picture.

Write out the alphabet on the chalkboard and encourage the children to memorise the sequence of letters. Now suggest that they think of different creatures beginning with a, b, c and so on. Make it a game, finding out how many

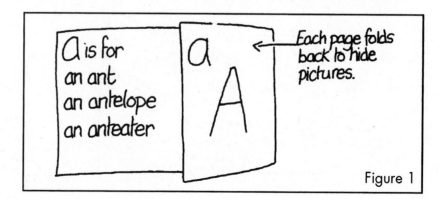

Figure 1

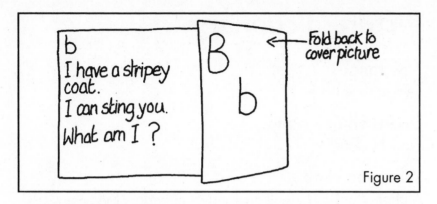

Fold back to cover picture

Figure 2

they can think of (don't worry if the children jump from letter to letter). This is an excellent exercise in key phonic.

Let the children use coloured pencils to write a letter of the alphabet on the fold-back at the right-hand side of each page. Next ask the children to write a clue to the creature on the left-hand side on the ruled line, either copying from the chalkboard or using their own independent writing, for example, for b: I have a stripy coat. I can sting you. What am I? (See Figure 2.)

They should then draw a picture of the creature in the space at the right of the page so that the picture will be hidden under the fold, as shown in Figure 3. Help the children to write the answer, for example, 'I am a bee', behind the fold.

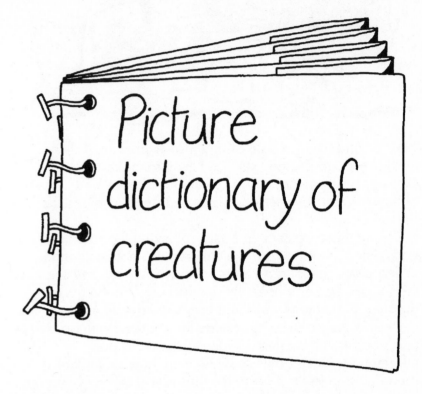

Figure 3

Once all the pages have been completed, let the children make a cover with the title, A Picture Dictionary of Creatures. Suggest that they draw a selection of creatures as a border.

Punch holes at the left-hand side of the pages and reinforce them. The finished dictionary can then be held together using treasury tags. Because of the folded-back pictures, the book will be much thicker at the right-hand side but, carefully handled, this picture dictionary should be a book to treasure.

Follow-up

• Suggest that the children try making a dictionary of names, of flowers or of places.
• Use the same technique to make word books. The books will need to be tall rather than long, so that the children can write a column of several words on each page.

Extension

This is the kind of book older children enjoy making for their younger brothers and sisters. For example, they could make a picture dictionary of characters from fairy tales or nursery rhymes.

Kaleidoscope of books

Once the children have had sufficient practice in designing and making a number of books in different styles and for different purposes, they will be ready to experiment with their newly-acquired bookmaking skills. They should be encouraged to exchange ideas and to work out how they might best express their own individuality through unusual or experimental ways of making books.

The ideas suggested below are interchangeable and some of the previously suggested books can be equally well produced in different formats, for example, four-page zigzags can become 'stage sets', flaps can be produced as pop-ups and sets of little books can be made to fit boxes and bags. One-poem books are particularly attractive, offering a means of combining artwork and writing in a very satisfying way. In this type of book, the artwork should reflect and enhance the content of the writing, for example, forest poems should be written inside or around a tree scene; sea poems should have the shape and colour of waves with fish and rock formations woven into the design.

To make the most of the books set out in this chapter you will need good quality cartridge paper, especially for those whose success depends on folds or pop-ups.

Day and night

Age range
Seven to eight.

You will need
A4 sheets of cartridge paper, scissors, pens or pencils, pencil crayons, chalkboard.

What to do
The purpose of this activity is to make a free-standing book with four sides, like a stage set. This method of presentation would be suitable for any writing/drawing activity which is divided into four scenes, such as times of the day (morning, afternoon, evening and night).

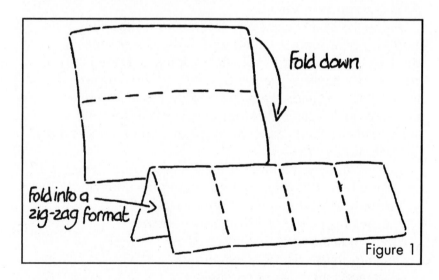

Figure 1

To make the 'stage set', take an A4 sheet and fold it lengthways, then fold it again into a double zigzag of four pages, as shown in Figure 1. Now cut along the top fold at the centre, pulling the middle section out sideways, so that it

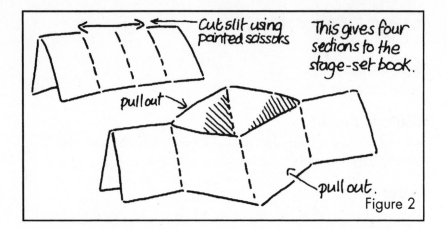

Cut slit using painted scissors

This gives four sections to the stage-set book.

pull out

pull out.

Figure 2

leaves a square space. (See Figure 2.) This makes a free-standing book with four separate two-page sections. Either show the children how to make the stage set or give each child one ready-made.

Divide the chalkboard into four sections, heading them morning, afternoon, evening and night. Discuss with the children what they are likely to be doing at these times of day and list some of the ideas. Now ask for suggestions about typical sounds we might hear in the morning (for example, milk bottles clinking, cars starting up), and at night (owls hooting, babies crying) and so on. Add these ideas to the list.

Suggest that the children use the lists to draft poems about each time of day, perhaps along the lines of:

Morning is waking-up and stretching
and getting your clothes on, yawn, yawn
Morning is the sound of milk bottles
clinking, mum calling, yawn, yawn.
Morning is the taste of cornflakes,
the smell of toothpaste, yawn, yawn.

Ask the children to draft an 'Afternoon is...', an 'Evening is...' and a 'Night is...' poem. Then let them write out the finished poems, one in each left-hand space on the stage set

books, and draw an appropriate scene on each right-hand page. Show them how to complete the one-book poem by using coloured pencil very lightly to colour behind the writing. Suggest that they colour the morning poem in pale pink, the afternoon in yellow, the evening in purple or blue and the night poem in grey.

The children could also use the stage set book for poems, stories or drawings about the four seasons, for example, 'An apple tree in spring, summer, autumn and winter', 'Clothes through the seasons', 'Games we play', and so on. The Nativity story could also be written in four scenes; Mary and the angel, the shepherds, the stable scene and the three kings. Again, they should use the left-hand page for the story, the right-hand section for artwork (Figure 3). A silver foil star could be stuck on above each scene to complete this book.

Follow-up

Read the poem 'Sea seasons' (given overleaf) with the children. Use this poem as a model to encourage the

The Kings

The stable scene

Mary and the Angel

The Shepherds

children to write a poem about 'Forest seasons', 'Mountain seasons', 'Meadow seasons'. The finished poems can be displayed in stage set books, a verse to each page and coloured with a faint coloured pencil to reflect the seasons.

Sea seasons

The sea bounces
over barnacles
bobbing and buckling
in the springtime breeze.

The sea prowls
over pebbles
pimpling and prickling
on damp autumn days.

The sea slithers
across shingle
splintering and sparkling
under a bright summer sun.

The sea rushes
across rocks
raging and raving
when winter winds blow.

Moira Andrew

The children could also write stories or poems set around the old rhyme, 'This year, next year, sometime, never'. The stage set idea is an ideal way of displaying this kind of work.

Books in a box

Age range
Eight to eleven.

What you need
Good quality paper to make mini-books, a selection of published mini-books, drafting paper, needle and cotton, pens, fine felt-tipped pens, fine card for the box, glue, sets of small books, chalkboard, hole punch, hole reinforcements, copy of photocopiable page 127.

What to do
Gather together as many small books as you can find and show them to the children; for example, a mini-Shakespeare set, Collins *Gem* guides, Collins *Nutshell Library*. Suggest to the children that they work on mini-books in a similar way.

Decide with the children whether this is to be a group or an individual project, and make a list of possible topics on the chalkboard. Ideas might include books about mini-beasts or a set of story books about the same character. (This last idea would be best suited to an individual writer.) These will make simple information books that young infants will be able to read for themselves.

Get the children to work on some sample ideas, for example, mini-beasts might be divided into 'crawling things' (worms, snails, caterpillars), 'flying things' (butterflies, dragonflies, bees, moths) and 'creeping things' (beetles, ants, earwigs).

Ask the children to begin by making some rough drafts so that they can match content to book/page size. Explain that they should draw and colour a creature for every page, carefully printing a name beneath the picture. Then get them to make appropriate covers.

Help the children to punch holes at the top and bottom

Figure 1

left-hand edge of each page and strengthen them with reinforcements. Show them how to use needle and cotton to thread through the holes, finishing off with a bow, as shown in Figure 1.

When the children have made several matching books, show them how to make a box the right size to keep them in. Use fine card, cut, folded and glued as shown in Figure 2, then decorate the box with felt-tipped pens or cut-out drawings of mini-beasts glued on collage-style. They might

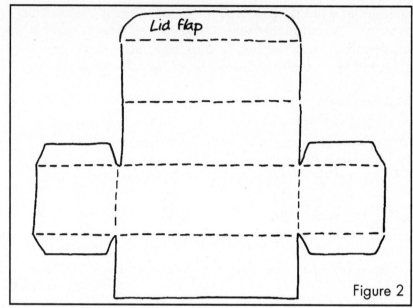

Figure 2

title the box *Mini-beast Mini-library*. A template for this is given on photocopiable page 127 which can be enlarged on a photocopier if necessary.

Those children who elect to write stories about a single character should make each little book the same size and shape, so that they too, can be kept in their own matching box.

Follow-up

The children could experiment with sweet-making, then make and write a set of mini-books of sweet recipes with their own matching box. To decorate the box, the children should cut out and mount pictures of coloured sweets, collage-style over the sides and top. Such mini-book sets make ideal presents for birthdays and Christmas.

The children could follow the same pattern to make a set of mini-books on gardening, decorating the box with cut-out flower pictures arranged collage-style.

Book in a bag

Age range
Eight to eleven.

What you need
Cartridge paper to make a small square book, needle and cotton, pens, felt-tipped pens or pencil crayons, fine card to make the bag, scraps of coloured wrapping paper, glue, narrow ribbon, scissors.

What to do
This idea works best when it is linked to a seasonal theme, for example, Mother's Day, Easter or Diwali.

Ask the children to write a poem to celebrate the festival, suggesting that the first lines use a pattern like this:

Easter is the colour of primroses,
yellow stars in the pale green grass.

Or:

Diwali is the colour of flames,
orange lights flickering in the darkness.

Next, ask the children to suggest how the festival would sound, taste, smell or feel with a last 'rounding up' couple of lines, giving six short stanzas altogether.

When writing a 'My mum' or 'My dad' poem, the children should use a similar pattern, for example:

My mum is like pink icing,
almost good enough to eat,
but when she gets mad at me
she's the colour of a ripe tomato!

Once the children have drafted the six verses of their poems, help them to make a small, double-fold book from two sheets of cartridge paper, approximately 160 x 80mm. This will make a square-shaped book of cover and six pages. Show the children how to sew the spine with

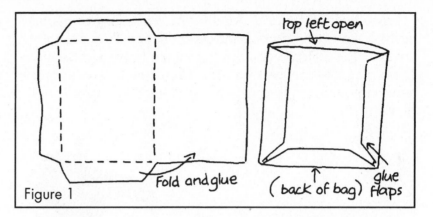

Figure 2

coloured cotton. Get them to write out the poem on the inside pages, taking a new page for each verse. The cover should then be decorated with felt-tipped pen or coloured pencil and each page should be illustrated.

Give the children fine card and scraps of coloured wrapping paper, then help them to make an open-topped bag, folding and sticking as shown in Figure 1. The bag should be made a few millimetres wider than the book. Let them attach ribbons to form handles, that slip the book inside, so that the top is just visible. (See Figure 2.)

Especially written and made for Mother's Day or another festival, the book in a bag makes a delightfully personal present. The children could also make a book in a bag to celebrate other family occasions, for example, the birth of a new baby, moving to a new house or celebrating a birthday.

Under the sea

Age range
Eight to eleven.

What you need
Sea music on tape (for example *Fingal's Cave*), sea pictures or posters, scrap paper, A4 card in blue or green, A4 paper, scissors, glue, pens, felt-tipped pens, a window letting in fairly bright light, pencils, frieze paper, silver foil.

What to do
Listen to the sea music tape together. Discuss with the children the sounds, the moods and the 'colours' of the music. Give out scrap paper and encourage the children to make notes on what they hear as they listen to the music for a second time.

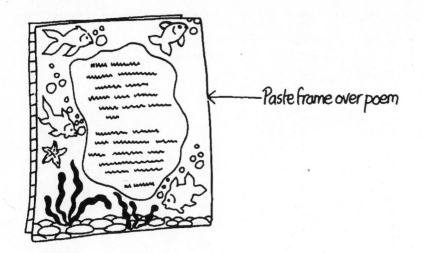

Paste frame over poem

Pin up a poster showing sea scenes and suggest that the children make a 'shopping list' of words and phrases inspired by the picture. Encourage them to use images, for example 'dolphins like arrows wounding the waves', 'seaweed like pale hands waving "good-bye"'.

Next ask the children to draft a poem based on their notes. Suggest that they go immediately into the poem, and make a point of banning such phrases as 'One day' or 'Once upon a time'. Explain that these tend to set the scene for stories and that this poem should be a sea picture in words, not a narrative.

When the children are happy with their poems, ask them to look carefully at the shape of the finished piece. Is it short and fat? Long and skinny? Does it have lines of different lengths?

Get them to write out their poems in the middle of a green or blue sheet of A4 card, making sure that the writing does not go too near the edge on either side. Next ask them to take their poems to a sunny window, and place a plain sheet of A4 paper over them, carefully matching the edges. Point out how the sun acts as a lightbox, enabling them to see the poem's outline through the top sheet, then get them to trace a wavy outline in pencil round the edge of the poem, to make a frame.

Ask the children to put their poems away while they work on the frame, using felt-tipped pens or coloured pencils to draw a sea environment. Once the frame is completed, help the children to cut out the middle part of the top sheet. Then let them fetch their written work and stick the sea picture frame in place over the poem. Suggest they edge the wave-shaped frame with a blue line to enhance the 'bubble' effect.

Display the poems on layered frieze paper in dark blues and greens with a touch of silver foil, again cut into curved wave shapes.

Follow-up

The frame technique works well for poems on a variety of different themes introduced in a similar way with music and picture starters. Try poems about space, lakes, mountains, forests or rainbows. The children should shape and colour the frames so that they are appropriate to the content of the poems.

Display the finished sea-poems on a wave background.

Use layers of blues, greens and some foil paper to make background.

Accordion books

Age range
Eight to eleven.

What you need
A long strip of sugar paper approximately 1 metre long x 30cm deep, card to make the cover, pens, felt-tipped pens, scissors, glue.

What to do
For this project, it is best to make the book first before the children decide on content. Help the children to fold the long strip of sugar paper as if they were making a double zigzag book, keeping the main fold at the top. They should then fold the zigzag into eight sections, keeping the end pages folded back as shown in Figure 1. Show the children

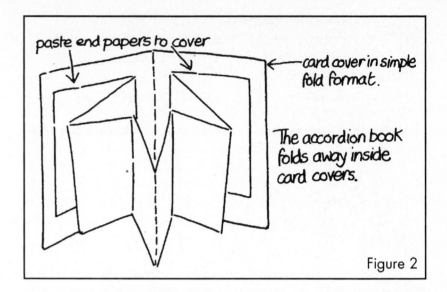

paste end papers to cover

card cover in simple fold format.

The accordion book folds away inside card covers.

Figure 2

how to stick the pages into a card cover, so that the finished book contains six pages which, unlike a zigzag, fold away completely inside its cover. (See Figure 2.)

Suggest that the children use the accordion book to display a mystery story. Explain that the story should be divided into three main sections with a major surprise occurring in each. For example, the story could take place in space. In part one, when the characters are travelling in the space ship, they might hear an unexpected sound from the engine. They could open the engine panel to find someone or something (a dog? a cat? a ghost? a favourite uncle?) who has come along for the ride.

In the second part of the story, after arriving on a planet (the moon? Saturn? Mars?), the travellers might look under a rock, open the door of an abandoned space-craft or dig a hole and uncover a surprise (a moonman? old bones? a treasure map?). When they return to earth, they could open the space-craft door to reveal the waiting press, a furious mum or that they have arrived back in the wrong place at the wrong time!

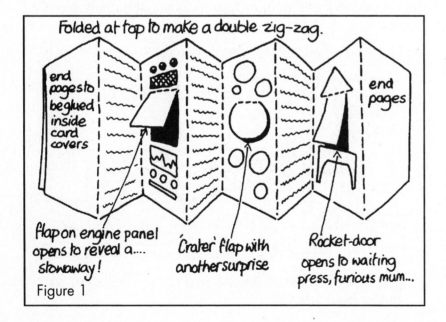

Folded at top to make a double zig-zag.

end pages to be glued inside card covers

end pages

Flap on engine panel opens to reveal a.... stowaway!

'Crater' flap with another surprise

Rocket-door opens to waiting press, furious mum...

Figure 1

Encourage the children to draft out a mystery story following the above outline, suggesting that it could take place on a treasure island, in an underground sewer or on the Orient Express. Explain that the first thing they must do is choose their scenario and the main characters.

When they are satisfied with their draft story, the children should write the story into the accordion book, two pages to each episode. Where a mystery occurs, the children should design a flap which can be raised to reveal the answer. For example, in the first part of the suggested space story, the children could show an engine panel, complete with knobs and dials. They could then cut round the illustration, so that it can be opened to reveal Great Uncle Harry hiding underneath. (See Figure 3.)

Children thoroughly enjoy working on the element of surprise which the accordion book offers. Furthermore the card covers of this type of book make it very durable and therefore of great value.

Follow-up

Junior children can use the accordion format to accommodate surprise stories written for younger children and non-readers.

end pages

Figure 3

Rag books

Age range

Eight to eleven.

What you need

White or cream cotton-type material, scraps of coloured cloth, needle and cotton, scissors and pinking shears, glue, a selection of simple picture books designed for babies.

What to do

Discuss with the children the characteristics of simple picture books, for example, one bold picture per page, no unnecessary detail, one word per page or no words at all. Ask the children to suggest how they might make books which would appeal to very young children. What safety factors would they need to take into account? (No staples, no painted surfaces and so on.)

Suggest that soft rag books might be best and ask the children to think of things that such a book might be about: toys, food, animals, pets, things around the house, flowers and so on. Ask them to choose their own category and

make rough drawings of what might go on each page, using simple bold outlines. For example, for the toy book they might suggest a ball, a teddy bear, a doll's house, a scooter.

Help the children to cut out a rag book from the white fabric, double-fold style, using pinking shears, then let them sew up the spine with thick cotton. Using their roughs as templates, the children should then trace the outline of the toys on to the scraps of coloured cloth. Ask the children to cut out the cloth pictures and stick them carefully into position in the rag book, one toy per page. Encourage the children to mix and match colours and patterns, so that, for example, a doll's house might have one pattern for the walls, another for the roof, dark blue cut-outs for windows and a bright red patch for the door.

Help the children to cut out fabric letters to make a title for the book, for example 'Toys', and sew them in position on the cover. The rag book would make a good present for a one-year-old brother or sister.

Follow-up
The children can make a rag book ABC or a rag book Nativity story. It is important to emphasise that the pictures should remain bold and simple for best effect.

What's in Polly's pocket?

Age range
Five to seven.

What you need
Cartridge paper, pens, scissors, a long-arm stapler and staples, chalkboard.

What to do
Introduce the character of Polly to the children. Explain that she is an untidy child who keeps an assortment of interesting things in her pockets. Ask the children to suggest items which Polly might have in her pocket and list them on the chalkboard. The list might include string, conkers, plastic spider, sweets, wrappers, elastic bands etc. Suggest that Polly's mother doesn't approve of her collection.

Explain that the children are going to make a counting book, so ask them to number the items for example:
• one plastic spider;
• two shiny conkers;
• three empty sweet wrappers, and so on.

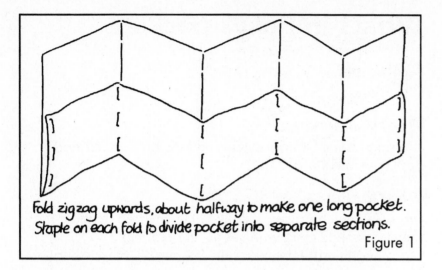

Fold zigzag upwards, about halfway to make one long pocket.
Staple on each fold to divide pocket into separate sections.

Figure 1

Help the children to make a zigzag book, folded upwards as shown in Figure 1, to make one long pocket. Staple the folds to divide the pocket into separate sections.

Get the children to write the title *What's in Polly's Pocket?* on the cover and number and name the pockets in sequence, as on their list. Then let them draw and cut out the spider, conkers, wrappers and so on, hiding the correct number in each pocket.

On the last page (the back cover), ask them to write a sentence beginning, 'and Mum said ...' and finish it appropriately.

Follow-up

Write a similar book on the theme of the question 'Where are Grandad's keys?'. Each page could offer an answer to the question, until the right answer is reached at the end of the book. For example:
- In his jacket pocket? No!
- In his trouser pocket? No!
- In his coat pocket? No!
- In his waistcoat pocket? Yes!

The squiggle-squoggle pocket book

Age range
Eight to eleven.

What you need
Cartridge paper or wrapping paper, felt-tipped pens, pens, double-sided adhesive tape, scissors, needle and cotton.

What to do
Suggest that the children create a 'squiggle-squoggle' monster, or allow them to use an equally alliterative name of their own choosing. Explain that this is a previously

undiscovered species, so they should invent a habitat for it, suggest what it would look like, what it would eat and what it would do all day. Encourage the children to be as zany as possible and first to draft their ideas in the style of a scientist describing a newly-discovered creature.

They might suggest something like this: 'The squiggle-squoggle has a purple-spotted coat, sharp red horns and a very fierce temper. He lives in the deepest muddiest swamp-lands and eats newts, frogs and any living creature with more than two legs that strays on to his private property.'

Help the children to make a small square book with pockets on each right-hand page. Let them use double-sided adhesive tape to make the pockets, as shown in Figure 1.

On the first left-hand page of the book, ask the children to write how the monster looks. Explain that on the next left-hand page, they should describe where the monster lives or what he eats, and so on until the book is filled.

Next ask them to make very tiny books to fit into each pocket. Suggest that the first tiny book should be 'The squiggle-squoggle's photograph album', and that they should draw 'photographs' of the monster, his mother, his baby brother, his uncle and aunt, and so on. Suggest that the next tiny book should show the monster's habitat, 'The squiggle-squoggle's ideal home'. The next pocket book could be 'The squiggle-squoggle's recipe book' or his diary. Explain that each tiny book should reflect the content of the left-hand page of the main book and should fit into its own pocket.

Follow-up

Invite the children to choose a mythical creature, such as a mermaid, unicorn, hobbit or troll, and write a poem about it. Explain that they should first list the parts of the creature, for example the unicorn would have a head, mane, tail, coat, horn and so on. Then suggest that the children use a combination of colour and image, for example: tail like an

Figure 1

Pocket book of presents

Age range
Five to eleven.

What you need
A3 sheets of cartridge paper, scissors, long arm stapler and staples or needle and cotton, pens, felt-tipped pens or coloured pencils, scissors, four small presents either made by the children or bought for a few pence (for example, pencil, ballpoint pen, packet of seeds, tube of peppermints, bookmark, photographs of the individual children).

What to do
This book makes an ideal Christmas or birthday gift for Grandma, Grandad or for mum on Mother's Day.

Give the children sheets of cartridge paper and get them to make a fold three quarters of the way up with the paper lengthways as in Figure 1. Then show them how to make

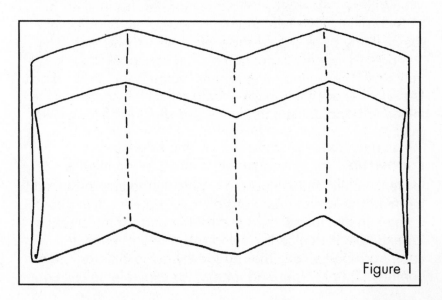

Figure 1

icy waterfall; horn like a vanilla ice-cream; coat the colour of newly-fallen snow, then encourage them to put these ideas together to make a 'designer' poem:

If I could design a unicorn,
I'd use the colours of winter.
For his tail I'd need an icy waterfall,
for his coat some newly-fallen snow.
I'd twirl his fantastic horn like an ice-cream cone.

Let the children make either a zigzag or a double-fold book, using a page for each line of the poem. Ask them to illustrate the poem as they go along. On the last page, suggest that the children make a pocket in which to hide the unicorn's diary, fact-file or a story book.

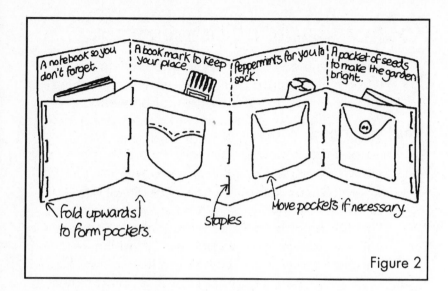

A notebook so you don't forget.

A book mark to keep your place.

Peppermints for you to suck.

A packet of seeds to make the garden bright.

fold upwards to form pockets.

staples

Move pockets if necessary.

Figure 2

zigzag folds to make four pages with a pocket on each (Figure 2). Let them sew or staple the paper, so that each pocket is quite separate.

Explain that the children should place a small present in each pocket, writing something appropriate in the space above. For example, if a child is making a pocket book of presents for Grandad, he could put in a notebook made from several sheets of paper sewn or stapled at the top, a coloured bookmark, a tube of peppermints and a packet of seeds. He could then write in the appropriate spaces, 'A notebook so you don't forget things', 'A bookmark to keep your place', 'Some peppermints for you to suck' and 'Nasturtium seeds to make the garden bright in summertime.' He could then put a message on the title page, such as 'A pocket book of presents for Grandad with lots of love from David.'

The children could make pockets of presents for other occasions. For example, they could include a poem, a recipe, some sweets and a photograph pasted into its own frame for a Mother's Day gift.

Rabbit's bad day

Age range
Eight to eleven.

What you need
Fine card to make a zigzag, scrap paper, scissors, cotton wool, fur fabric, needle and cotton, felt-tipped pens, strong glue, fabric scraps, copies of photocopiable page 128.

What to do
Suggest that the children draft a simple story of four episodes in which Rabbit has a hard time. Explain that they should make it suitable for a very young audience and that it is important that Rabbit should find several hiding places. Read them the following story as an example:

Part 1: One day Rabbit went for a walk in the woods. He heard a strange noise and hid behind a bush. It was only a crow, so Rabbit went on.
Part 2: Then he saw a man with a gun, so he hid behind a rock. When the man had gone, Rabbit went on.
Part 3: He looked to left and right, but didn't look where he was going. SPLASH! Rabbit fell into the pond! 'I wish I was home,' he said to himself.
Part 4: So Rabbit bobbed through the long grass until he came to his own burrow. 'What has happened to you, Rabbit?' asked his mother. 'I've had a bad day!' said Rabbit. So mum dried him off and put Rabbit to bed.

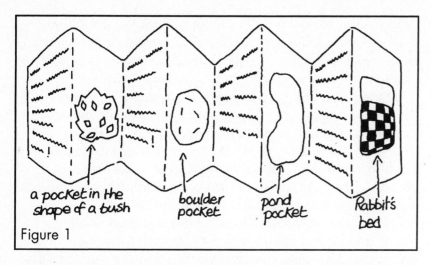

a pocket in the shape of a bush

boulder pocket

pond pocket

Rabbit's bed

Figure 1

Give the children copies of photocopiable page 128 and ask them to cut out the rabbit template. Show them how to use it as a pattern to cut two matching shapes from the fur fabric. Explain that they should put the two pieces together and sew almost the whole way round the edge, before stuffing it with cotton wool and sewing up the hole. Suggest that they make eyes and whiskers on the face, either by sticking on fabric shapes or by drawing with felt-tipped pen, and make a cotton wool tail and stick it on.

Next, ask the children to fold a length of card into a zigzag with eight inside pages. Ask them to write on the title page *Rabbit's Bad Day*, then use their draft stories to write out their rabbit story into the zigzag on the left-hand pages only. Tell them to take a new page for each episode.

When the children have written the story neatly into the zigzag they should cut out Rabbit's various hiding places from fabric scraps. Ask them to paste or sew these on to the right-hand pages, making 'pockets' for Rabbit. Explain that the idea is that the young reader is able to move Rabbit from place to place as the story progresses. (See Figure 1.) Young readers will enjoy the interactive element in this type of book.

Follow-up

Once the children have constructed one story like this, they could be invited to make more complicated pocket books full of imaginative hiding places for their main character. A cat or a teddy could be hidden in a flower pot, a basket, a box, behind a cushion and so on, giving both writers and readers a great deal of enjoyment.

119

Haunted house pop-up

Age range
Eight to eleven.

What you need
Fine card, scissors or a craft knife and self-sealing board, pens, felt-tipped pens.

What to do
Pop-up books offer pure enjoyment for the children, in addition, of course, to encouraging more advanced design and book-making skills.

Suggest to the children that they work on a simple story outline involving the appearance of ghosts and monsters; a haunted house or castle would provide an excellent background. Ask them to work on a draft before beginning the book. Encourage the children to make their first effort fairly simple so that they can master the mechanics of the pop-up.

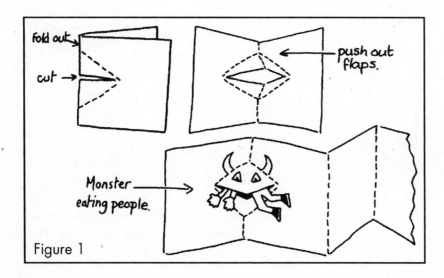

Figure 1

Suggest that they write a simple opening to the story, such as 'We visited the haunted house for a dare. "Creak", we opened the door and out jumped a monster that had just had lunch. Legs hung from its bright red mouth!'

Let them use fine card to make a zigzag with an even number of pages. Then suggest that the children make the monster's mouth inside the first zigzag fold, as shown in Figure 1. Ask them to draw the monster over the double page (around its mouth), making it look as weird as possible. They can finish the effect by adding disembodied legs and feet hanging from the monster's mouth.

On the next fold the children could design a floating ghost, and on the next one draw a monster. For these more complicated cut-outs, the children might find it easier to use a craft knife (always on a self-sealing board for safety) instead of scissors.

On the back cover, ask the children to draw two tiny figures fleeing from the haunted house with speech bubbles saying, for example, 'You won't catch me back there! Not even for a dare!' The front cover should have the title *The Haunted House* printed in wobbly bubble writing.

Follow-up
• For more complicated stories, the children could make the zigzag longer, alternating each pair of pages, so that two carry the storyline and the following two have a pop-up character. Suggest that the children contour the book's top in the shape of a castle.
• The children could write space stories with pop-up characters showing aliens and spacemen.
• They could write pop-up stories for younger children, with animal pop-ups hiding in a woodland scene.
• They could write underwater stories where the characters include sharks with teeth, King Neptune, mermaids and assorted creatures of the deep.

What's over the fence?

Age range
Eight to eleven.

What you need
Fine card, staples and stapler or needle and cotton, pointed scissors, pens, felt-tipped pens.

What to do
Ask the children to curl their fingers and look at familiar things around them through the tiniest hole possible. Point out how when they see only part of a picture, things are often not what they seem. For example, the branches of a bare tree might look like a hedgehog's bristles, a rainbow like a scrap of ribbon, the centre of a daisy like the sun and so on. Encourage the children to think of imaginative ideas.

Ask the children to make a double-fold book, sewn or stapled along the spine, and explain that this book is intended to be read by the youngest children in the school and that there should be a question and answer on every page. The book should be titled *What's Over the Fence?* and the cover should show children on tip-toe trying to see through a hole near the top of a tall fence.

Ask the children to continue the fence illustration across all the pages of the book, making it lower on each successive page. Suggest that on each right-hand page they should cut a hole, with something unusual visible through it; for example, a scrap of rainbow with the question 'Is it a ribbon?' and the answer, 'No, it's a rainbow!' Explain that the children will need to work carefully on the design of this book, making sure that each successive hole is lower than the one on the previous page.

Follow-up
The children could make more books with holes, using different designs. They can make holes for younger children to put their fingers through to make, for example, a rabbit's ears or a spider's legs.

Reproducible material

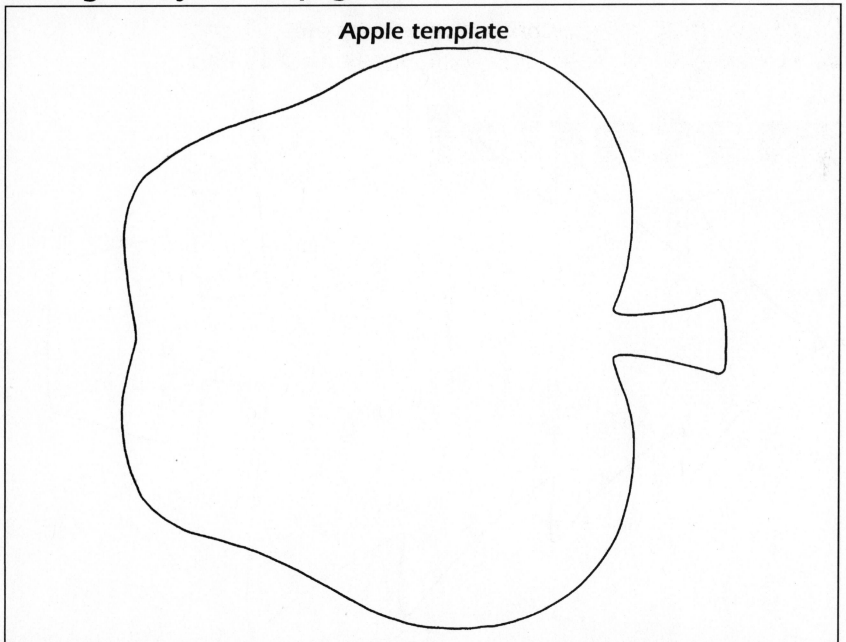

Apple template

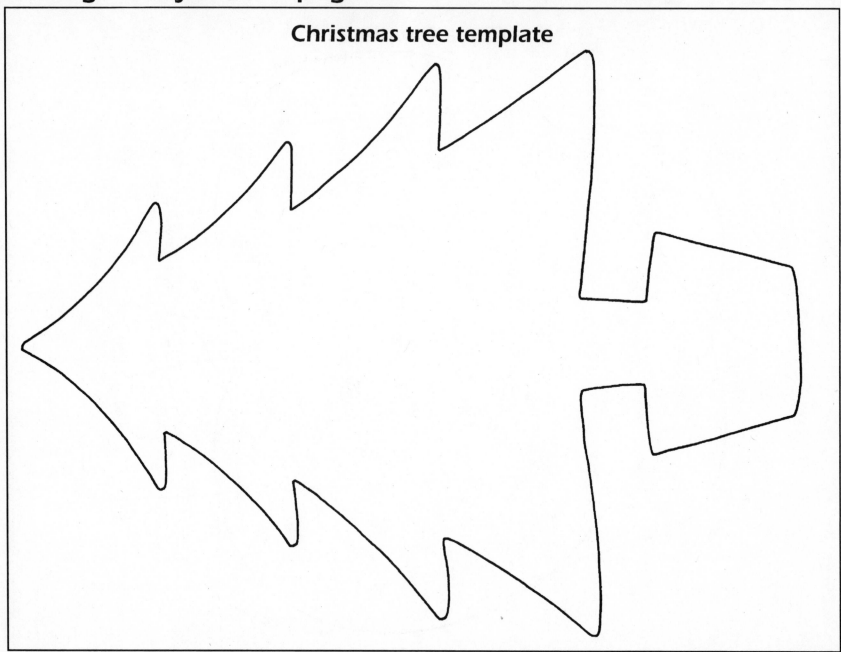

Christmas tree template

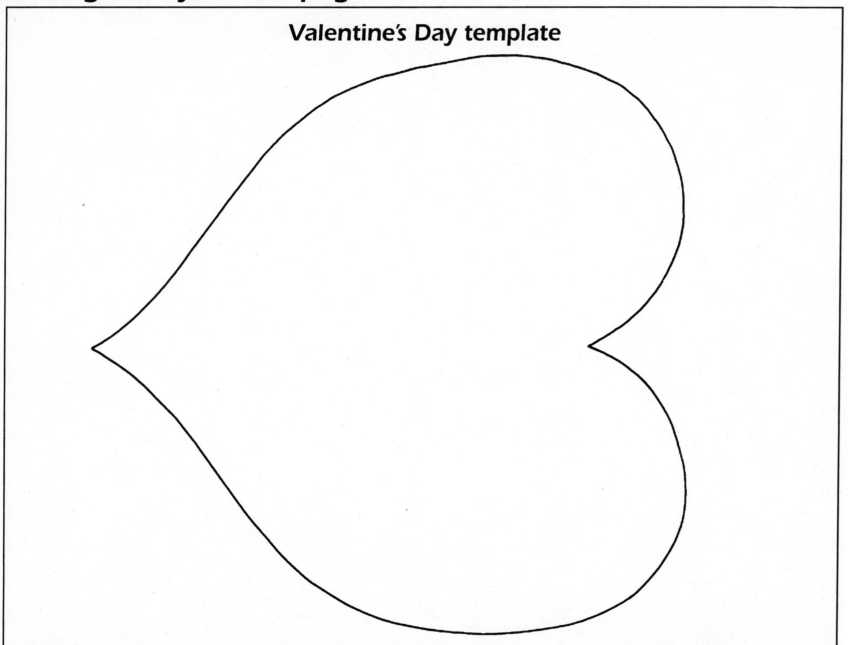

Valentine's Day template

Through the year, see page 55

Remembrance poppy template

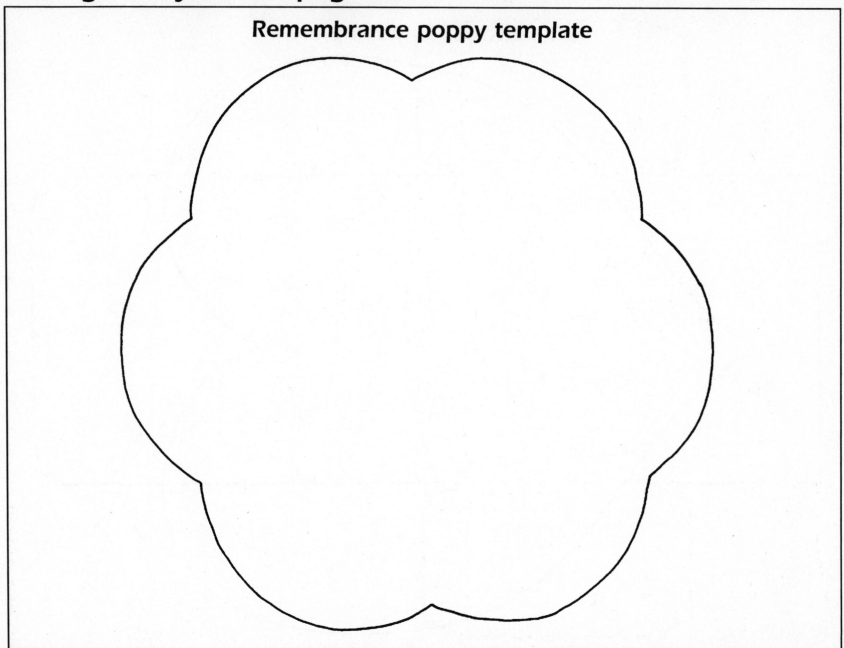

This page may be copied for use in the classroom and should not be declared in any return in respect of any photocopying licence.

Books in a box, see page 105

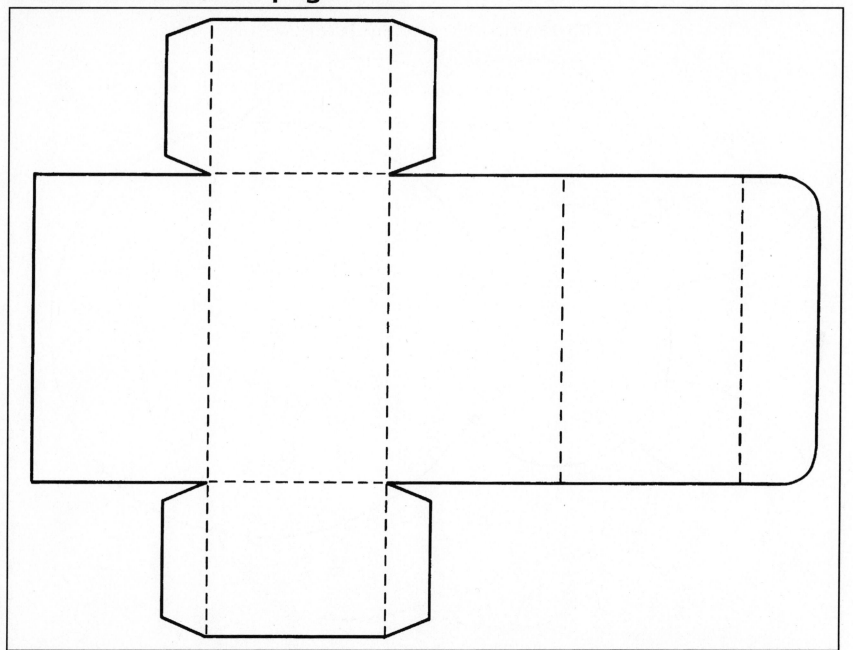

Rabbit's bad day, see page 118

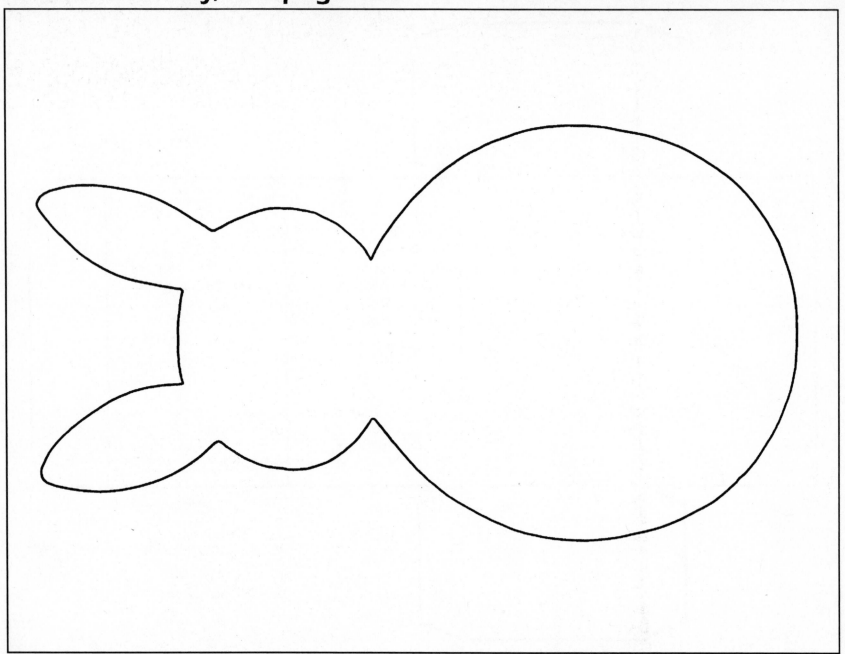